The Massachusetts Gardener's Companion

Gardener's Companion Series

The Massachusetts Gardener's Companion

*An Insider's Guide to Gardening
from the Berkshires to the Islands*

Barbara Gee

The
Globe
Pequot
Press

GUILFORD, CONNECTICUT

The information in this book has been carefully researched. The author and publisher assume no liability for accidents happening to, injuries sustained, or any damage, loss, or inconvenience incurred by the reader as a result of following the information in this book. When using any commercial product, always read and follow label directions. Mention of a trade name does not imply endorsement by the publisher.

Copyright © 2007 by Morris Book Publishing, LLC

Text design by Casey Shain
Illustrations by Josh Yunger
Map by M. A. Dubé © Morris Book Publishing, LLC

Library of Congress Cataloging-in-Publication Data
Gee, Barbara.
  A Massachusetts gardener's companion : an insider's guide to gardening from the Berkshires to the islands / Barbara Gee. — 1st ed.
      p. cm.—(Gardener's companion series)
    Includes index.
    ISBN-13: 978-0-7627-4309-4
    ISBN-10: 0-7627-4309-3
  1. Gardening—Massachusetts. I. Title. II. Series.
    SB451.34.M4G44 2007
    635.09744—dc22
                                                                    2006035412

Manufactured in the United States of America
First Edition/First Printing

To Julie Morris, my friend and mentor,
and to Jeffrey, Samara, and Danya

Contents

Introduction

To say that Massachusetts is a diverse state is an understatement to be sure. Covering approximately 10,555 square miles (7,800 of them land), Massachusetts is bordered south, southeast, and east by the Atlantic Ocean and inland by five New England states. The terrain is pretty flat in the southeast, close to the ocean, but it starts to rise as you move west through the geographic center of the state in Worcester County to the higher elevations of the Taconic Range. Apart from the island counties of Dukes and Nantucket, the state has an ocean coast of about 250 miles. Plymouth County alone has swamps, beaches, dunes, tidal marshes, and the largest area of peat in the state. Massachusetts has it all—which is great for the tourism industry but can be daunting when addressing gardening issues. Generalizations just don't cut it!

How often have you lamented, "I love this plant but it just won't survive here" or "I love that magazine, but half the articles are about plants we can't grow." *The Massachusetts Gardener's Companion* addresses the specifics of gardening in Massachusetts— its soil, climate, hardiness zones, growing conditions, challenges, and special places. Throughout this book you will find some great plant recommendations from Massachusetts gardeners, terrific tips for helping your plants thrive, and a chapter of state-specific resources from which you can gather yet more information to make your gardening endeavors a success. A glossary and index round out the book.

Although I came to gardening a little later in life, when my husband and I moved from a condominium in Brookline to a house, I learned to garden *fast*. I enrolled in the master gardener program and then continued my studies with the Royal Horticultural Society's course for certification in horticulture. I then worked at a retail nursery, followed by a stint with a landscape designer, and (my favorite) worked in the department of horticulture at Blithewold Mansion, Gardens & Arboretum in Bristol, Rhode Island.

From my years writing about gardening in New England and as a state editor for the Northeast gardening magazine *People, Places & Plants*, I have gained a deeper appreciation of the topographic and climate differences in the Bay State. My special love is city gardens (especially those in Brookline, Newton, Beacon Hill, Newburyport, and Marblehead) and seaside gardens like those on Cape Cod and the Islands. You'll read about these in chapter 11. And these days I explore the gardens of central Massachusetts around the University of Massachusetts in Amherst, where one of my daughters is studying.

Many generous folks have shared their knowledge of Massachusetts gardening to make *The Massachusetts Gardener's Companion* a really useful resource. Space constraints prohibit my thanking them all by name, but you will find them quoted throughout the book. To each one I extend my gratitude.

I hope this book provides you with recommendations and resources that will be useful wherever you garden in the Bay State. Write to me with your suggestions and comments care of The Globe Pequot Press, P.O. Box 480, Guilford, CT 06437-0480.

Firm
Foundations

Soils

As you stride across your lawn, do you stop to think about what's going on beneath your feet? Soil should be alive, teeming with activity—rich and abundant in microbes, insects, nutrients, moisture, and air. Soil that has been depleted of life is a sorry thing to behold—pale, gray, dry, literally lifeless, with not a worm to be seen.

Poor soil contributes to 80 percent of plant growing problems. Knowing your soil and knowing exactly how to improve it is vital to gardening success.

Gardening is an act of collaboration between you and Mother Nature. As with any relationship, if you want the collaboration to be fruitful, it helps to know with whom or what you're dealing. To get the most out of your little patch of earth, take a moment and consider the bigger picture: why we have the soil we have in Massachusetts, where it came from, how it was formed, and if it is good or bad. Good soil is the foundation of gardening success, so let's look at it in depth.

What Is Soil?

Soil begins with the breakdown of rocks into small mineral particles by environmental factors: wind, rain, heat, and cold. Factor in the accumulation of decaying organic materials such as leaves and grass; the chemistry that happens when roots move through the soil; the activity of organisms such as microbes, insects, earthworms, and humans attacking organic matter; the topography of the land; and time. The end result is soil.

Good soil is essential to plant health. It is a support for plants, holding them in place. It provides plants with the nutrients, moisture, and air (oxygen) they need. To do all of this well, the soil must be balanced: composed of the correct proportions of minerals, nutrients, air, water, and beneficial insects and animals. Good soil holds enough water for the plants' needs yet drains well enough that the plants and animal life don't suffocate. We're not all blessed with good soil on our property—but we can create it.

A well-balanced surface soil is made up of approximately half solid material and half open spaces. Some of the soil particles are big enough to see easily, while others are so small you'd need a microscope to view them. Most soils are classified based on the amount of clay, sand, or silt they contain and are usually a combination of these mineral elements in different amounts.

- Gravel or sand particles are the largest. They don't hold water well but let air into the soil.
- Clay particles are very small and can compact, which means that water does not drain through efficiently and air can't get in easily.
- Silt particles are medium size, in between sand and clay.

Clay soils, like those found in the Connecticut River valley, are heavy to work and slow to drain but can be very fertile. They are slow to warm up in the spring. Clay soils hold water too well and become waterlogged and compacted, which makes it hard for plants to get access to either air or water. Clay soils shouldn't be worked when wet because they can be easily damaged. When dry they tend to shrink. One advantage of clay soil is that it holds high levels of nutrients; however, the nutrients aren't easily available to the plants. Clay soil requires good management to make the nutrients available.

Sandy soils, which are found through most of Massachusetts, have low levels of nutrients and lose nutrients fairly fast due to fast drainage. These soils have less clay in them and therefore hold less water. Sandy soils usually have low levels of organic matter, but any organic matter that is added will break down quickly and improve the texture. Sandy soil warms up quickly in the spring and is easy to work when wet. When dry it can be dusty and difficult to handle.

Silty soils are not commonly found in Massachusetts. They are fairly easy to work when dry, but like sandy soils they can be dry and dusty. They are less easy to work when wet and tend to compact easily. Silty soils are slow to warm up in the spring. They have only moderate levels of organic matter and nutrients. Water is easily absorbed into these soils but can contribute to erosion.

Soils can range from gravelly sand to loamy sand to sandy loam to silt loam and to silty clay loam, clay loam, sandy clay, sandy clay loam—and so on.

Soils in Massachusetts

"There's perhaps no better place to study soils than Massachusetts," says Steven Bodine of the Soil and Plant Tissue Testing Laboratory at the University of Massachusetts in Amherst. "Our closeness to the southernmost advance of the last glaciation, together with our wide range of rock types and subtle yet significant variations in climate, have resulted in a rich variety of soils."

Massachusetts is primarily glacial till, which is made up mostly of sand (40 to 60 percent) and silt (30 to 35 percent). The remainder is clay. *Glacial* simply means "moved by ice," and *till* means a mix of sand, silt, and clay. Sandy loams are typical of glacial till.

Dipping your hand into your soil is literally touching prehistory. Massachusetts soils are the result of the most recent ice age, which reached its maximum development 20,000 years ago, when the whole state was covered with a glacier. The ice started to retreat 12,000 to 14,000 years ago, moving through central Massachusetts 10,000 years ago. And move it did, pushing soils around and rearranging the land like a bulldozer. As the ice melted it washed soil materials away from the northern hills toward the ocean. You'll hear the term "outwash" used to describe these soils.

The soils in Massachusetts are termed "young soils" because they are only 10,000 to 12,000 years old, versus millions of years old in the Southeast. If glaciation had not occurred, then Massachusetts soil would more closely resemble the red clay of the southeast United States. In some places, usually toward the Cape, you can sometimes find clues as to what the soil was like originally. If you see large boulders in your area, or lots of stone walls, chances are the soil was glacial in origin. "The moving glacial meltwaters carried the big boulders and stones here," says Cape Cod landscape designer Paul Miskovsky.

"While one can state that Massachusetts soils are stony sandy loams or loamy sands, there are localized pockets of stone-free finer textured soils derived from river, wind, and ocean

The State Soil

In 1922 Massachusetts soils were mapped and the term "Paxton soil" was coined after the town of Paxton in Worcester County. Then in 1991 the Massachusetts State Legislature designated the Paxton fine sandy loam as the official state soil of the Commonwealth. Paxton soil is well drained, with a high water-holding capacity. It is coarse and loamy, formed from acid glacial till mostly derived from granite, gneiss, and schist. These soils are found throughout southern New England and Massachusetts except Cape Cod, Martha's Vineyard, and Nantucket. The primary agricultural crops for Paxton soils are apples, corn, and silage, according to the Natural Resources Conservation Service. The trees you find thriving will typically give a good indication of the type of soil: Trees commonly found growing on these soils include red, white, and black oak; hickory; sugar and red maple; gray and black birch; white pine; and hemlock.

deposits," notes Steven Bodine. "The best examples of these are found in the Connecticut River valley. These soils are easy to till and have near perfect drainage. Farmers love them."

What about *your* soil? In general terms you can learn about the different soils in Massachusetts by referring to counties. You can research the soil surveys for your county's soil from the Natural Resources Conservation Service at www.nrcs.usda.gov. A quick survey reveals the differences.

Berkshire County, for instance, has two sorts of soils—those in the uplands and those in the valleys. Hoosic River and Housatonic River valley soils are derived from limestone bedrock. In the uplands the soils are primarily of glacial origin; in the lowlands soils are of fluvial origin, which means moved by water. Because of the high elevations, cold temperatures, and weathering patterns, upland soil is quite different from lowland soil. The higher the elevation, the greater the weathering effect. There you'll find northern mountain trees growing. On 3,491-foot Mount Greylock, for instance, are trees typical of those found in southern Canada: red oak, hemlock, red spruce, and balsam fir.

Hampshire County's lowlands are dominated by the Connecticut River valley. After the glacier receded, a large earthen dam remained, blocking the whole valley. As the waters melted they couldn't get past the dam. A huge lake formed there and all the way up to New Hampshire. Some of the soils left in this lake area are silty clay loams and clay loams, but they are some of the best soils in the state.

Essex County has the only clay-rich soils in the state. As the glacier receded it pushed the ground into a depression. The land took a while to rebound. While it was depressed, seawater came in, depositing marine clay. This fertile marine clay loam lines the area. If the drainage is good, it can be an excellent growing medium. The pH of this soil is close to neutral (7.0), which is also unusual for the state. (See the information on soil pH later.)

Cape Cod and the Islands offer an unusual mix of soils.

Martha's Vineyard and Nantucket exist because of glacier movement. As the ice bulldozed its way across Narragansett Bay, it shifted the land, lifting it up to create these areas. The glacier deposited materials it had picked up along its path. The soil in these areas is sandy with a lot of gravel and cobbles, low in silt and clay content.

Although the Cape is dominated by sandy tills and outwash, even there you'll find areas where small lakes formed, leaving glacier-deposited clays. You will also find landforms called kettle holes on the Cape. These are large depressions in the land left by the ice. They can be as large as 23,000 square feet and as deep as 25 feet below grade. Some are still full of water, which renders them a pond or lake.

Martha's Vineyard and Nantucket are located near the end of all the glacier movement, so there you'll find more of this loamy glacial till and outwash with some leftover material from preglacial weathering periods. John Bartlett of Bartlett's Farm on Nantucket says that he farms on what's known as "riverhead sandy loam soils."

Worcester County in the center of the state has finer-textured rocks, resulting in a whole range of loam through sand. You'll also find some of this in Berkshire County.

Physical Properties of Soil

All soil is composed of three layers, known as horizons. You may have seen the three layers if you've dug down deeply or looked closely at a construction site.

Topsoil is the top horizon. It is darker because it contains organic content. Most root action takes place in this layer, and that's why plants obtain most of their water and nutrients from this surface horizon.

Subsoil, the next layer down, is lighter in color and less fertile. There's less root growth in this layer.

Parent material is the third layer—bedrock in the case of Massachusetts. Roots cannot penetrate this layer.

No matter what its makeup, soil is described in terms of its physical properties: texture, color, and structure.

Texture: You probably won't be able to truly identify what soil texture you have without a soil test (see the soil testing section later in the chapter), but you can quickly get a rough idea by taking some soil in your hand and rubbing it between your fingers. Sandy soil will feel gritty and won't hold together; a clay soil will remind you of pottery class—sticky, heavy, and easy to mold into a ball. Silty soil has a silky, slippery feel in your hand. You can go through complicated tests yourself with jars of water watching how the soil separates, but the most efficient way is to send soil samples off to a lab. A soil test is essential to find out the exact texture and also the accurate pH of your soil.

Color: A soil's color is an indication of how much organic material that soil contains. The darker the color the greater the organic matter content. If the soil is light, it usually indicates that

Do You Have Good Topsoil?

When you buy a home, find out what the soil is like around the house. In new developments, contractors often remove the topsoil and sell it, leaving the home buyer with nothing but subsoil. Or your home may be built on an old potato field, or similar, and the soil may have been depleted of its nutrients. At the Conway School of Landscape Design in Conway, landscape architect Jean Aker teaches about the issue of poor soils. "Many former hillsides were overfarmed and lost their topsoil 150-plus years ago," she says. "If the depth and structure isn't there due to either of these past events, any gardener will continue to struggle with limited success in poor soil conditions."

What Is Loam?

Really good soil is a dark, chocolatey brown or black, which indicates that it has a high content of organic material. It is slightly crumbly in texture and healthy smelling, with no foul odors. It has good texture, good drainage, and the right amounts of moisture and air. This is loam—a balanced mix of sand, silt, and clay. Loam is good soil that holds water well yet drains well so that air can reach the roots. It is sandy enough that water drains from it but with enough clay to retain water. What if you don't have this loamy perfection? There are ways to get your soil as close to loam as possible. See "Improving Soil" later in the chapter.

the soil is light in organic matter, either through excessive drainage or overuse, which has depleted the soil.

Structure: Soil structure, or tilth, is the soil's physical condition. "Tilth" comes from the Old English word for cultivating soil. A soil is said to have good tilth, or to be "friable," if it has a structure that holds together if compressed and yet crumbles easily, if it absorbs water quickly, and if the water drains easily.

Soil Chemistry, Soil pH

Nutrients become available to plants when those nutrients are dissolved in the soil. The acidity of a soil determines how well nutrients dissolve and therefore become available. If your soil is either too acid or alkaline, nutrients are either completely unavailable because they are not dissolved, or they dissolve too slowly to be useful to plants.

The term pH means potential hydrogen. It is a measurement of how alkaline or acid the soil is. The pH measurements range from 1 to 14:

- The lower end is acid: 1 to 5. Lemons have a pH of 1.3 to 2.4.

- The high end is alkaline: 8 to 14. Ammonia has a pH 10.6 to 11.6.

- Neutral pH is in the middle: 6 to 7. Pure water has a pH of 7.

A soil pH somewhere in the range of 6 to 7 will cause most plant nutrients to be available to the plants. Most Massachusetts soils are generally acidic, with a pH somewhere between 5.0 and 5.8. It is generally low in nutrients because of the type of igneous rocks from which it was formed. Massachusetts gardeners probably won't encounter alkaline soil.

It's important to measure the acidity of your soil so you know when to make improvements and when to leave well enough alone. Soil pH also affects the activity of beneficial microorganisms. The work of bacteria on the decomposition of organic matter can be slowed down or stopped entirely in highly acidic soils. What you end up with is organic matter that cannot decompose. This does nothing to improve your soil and it may cause problems like poor drainage, poor aeration, or the accumulation of harmful bacteria.

Changing Your Soil pH

If your soil is too alkaline, which is rarely the case in Massachusetts, you will want to add sulfur to lower the pH level. If your soil is too acid, you'll want to add lime to raise the pH level. Lime requirements vary with soil type. The higher the organic content of a soil, the more lime it will take to bring about a change in pH. Lime increases nitrogen availability because it speeds up the decomposition of organic matter. Adding lime does more than just raise the level of pH in your soil—it also adds calcium and magnesium to the soil and helps make phosphorus more available to the plants. The addition of lime also reduces the risk of aluminum and manganese toxicity that can occur in soil with a low pH.

Monitor your soil to make sure you're not adding too much lime. Some common liming materials are dolomitic limestone (helpful where magnesium levels are low), bonemeal, ground shells, and wood ashes from your fireplace. Wood ashes sweeten your soil, says landscape designer Katie Haried of Newburyport. "One

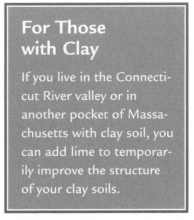

always needs to add lime here, so I've learned that a fast way to get lime into the soil is to spread the ashes from my fireplace." A note of caution: Make sure the ashes are truly cool. A friend of mine set her garden on fire because there were still warm coals in the ashes!

Raising or lowering the pH of your soil depends somewhat on the soil you have: sand or clay. A simple rule of thumb: To raise the pH one unit, mix in anywhere from two to nine pounds of limestone per 100 square feet. To lower the pH one unit, add sulfur at the rate of two to five pounds per 100 square feet.

pH Preferences

The pH range that you will be working with for most plants is between 4.5 and 7.0. But you have to know what your plants want before attempting to change the pH. Here are examples of plant pH preferences:
- Rhubarb—6.0 to 7.0
- Turnips—5.5 to 6.8
- Potatoes—5.0 to 6.5
- Sweet corn—5.5 to 7.5
- Sweet potatoes—5.2 to 6.0
- Bentgrass—5.5 to 6.5

Testing Your Soil

Even assuming that your Massachusetts soil is acid, you'll still want to know what range of acidity it falls within. The most accurate method of determining your soil's pH level is to get a soil test performed at a lab (see the "Soil Test Sources" sidebar). There are, however, pH meters on the market that you can stick directly into the garden or into a soil sample that you've collected. You can also buy a soil pH testing kit, which usually comes with litmus paper and a color chart. You add soil to a little water and put the litmus paper into the solution. The paper changes color and you check it against the color chart to match it up with the color of your pH level.

The soil pH may vary in different pockets of your property. Don't assume that one test will give you all the information you need. Get several tests done from samples around your yard.

Sending soil off for testing is easy. Detailed instructions are provided on the form you submit with your sample, but in simple terms you take a sample of soil anywhere from 3 to 8 inches down

Soil Test Sources

Soil tests can be performed at a private lab or a state facility. A good Web site to locate a private lab is www.attra.ncat.org/attra-pub/soil-lab. Private labs are usually more expensive than going to a state facility, however. The University of Massachusetts Extension Service offers a variety of soil and compost tests for a relatively small fee. Get details at www.umass.edu/plsoils/soiltest or write to the Soil and Plant Tissue Testing Laboratory, West Experiment Station, 682 North Pleasant Street, University of Massachusetts, Amherst, MA 01003. You can often find the UMass Amherst brochure and soil sample kits in local garden centers.

and send the soil in with the fee. Identify it for your own reference, particularly if you send in more than one sample.

Depending on the test you request, the soil test results will reveal the soil pH, buffer pH, extractable nutrients (such as nitrogen, iron, zinc), soil texture, soluble salts, and others.

When is the correct time to do a soil test? It depends on when you want the results. You can do a soil test in early fall to get results back in time to add amendments before winter, so the amendments can then do their work over the winter. Or you can test in the spring before you start planting so you can make improvements to the soil without disturbing what's to be planted. It's virtually impossible to take soil samples when the soil is hard or frozen.

Improving Soil

Building up your soil is exactly like building up your own health—the stronger you are the easier it is to fight off sickness and disease, the more cheerful you are, and the more receptive you are to all things in life. It's the same for soil.

Plants need seventeen elements for normal growth. Fourteen of these come from the soil: boron, calcium, chlorine, cobalt, copper, iron, nitrogen, magnesium, manganese, molybdenum, phosphorus, potassium, sulfur, and zinc. The other three are carbon, hydrogen, and oxygen: Carbon comes from carbon dioxide; hydrogen and oxygen come from the water in the soil.

Of these, the three major elements are nitrogen (N), phosphorus (P), and potassium (K).

You will see the "N-P-K" ratio on many products, including fertilizers. Each element has its own growing characteristic, but the combination of the three affects the speed of growth, the size of flower blossoms, the size and amount of fruit, the shade of green, and the strength of the stem. Nitrogen, for instance, gives a plant its dark green color and increases the growth of leaves and stems. Phosphorus stimulates the early formation and strong growth of roots, and potassium increases a plant's resistance to disease. A deficiency or excess of any of these elements will cause problems. Lack of nitrogen may result in light green to yellow leaves, and lack of potassium may result in small fruit or thin skin.

The Importance of Organic Matter

Perhaps you need to improve your soil's pH level, texture, nutrient content, amount of air, or the water retention. Or maybe you need to remedy a lack of beneficial organisms like earthworms or too many harmful organisms like grubs or nematodes. You can achieve almost all of these improvements simply by adding organic matter.

Organic matter is made up of decomposed plant and animal material, or humus—great stuff for the garden. Organic material stays in the soil and keeps on working to improve it year after year. Plants can make use of the nutrients released from organic materials more easily because nutrients are released at a rate and in a way the plants can efficiently absorb them.

Incorporate an amendment into the soil by digging it in or using it as topdressing or mulch—a lot depends on how deep you want to get the material. Be aware that amendments will not work their garden magic if the soil is cold. The chemistry begins when the soil temperature goes above 40 degrees.

Here's a closer look at commonly available amendments:

Animal manure is a wonderful amendment, but you have to be careful when using it. Don't use animal manure on plants you intend to eat because of the possible transference of disease pathogens. Manure must be aged. Fresh manure can be too strong and burn plants. It may also contain viable weed seeds. Get your manure from a trusted source. Aged manure should not have an unpleasant odor. Manures are designated "hot" or "cold" depending on the amount of nitrogen and fluid content: Cow and pig manures are cold; horse, sheep, and hen manures are hot.

Organic slow-release fertilizers with names like Earth Juice and Cockadoodle Doo are excellent amendments. They add minerals other than just nitrogen, phosphorus, and potassium. Their N-P-K ratio will be more in the range of 5-3-3 or 4-2-3 instead of the 10-10-10 you commonly find in synthetic fertilizers. The numbers are lower, but this is not an indication of the power of these products.

Why use organic fertilizers instead of the less-expensive chemical forms? Synthetic or chemical fertilizers don't improve the soil long term in the many ways organic material and organic fertilizers do. "Chemical fertilizers are a quick fix," says Bruce Thompson, the Massachusetts state soil scientist. "Putting organic matter back into the soil and improving it is much better." And improving your soil is the goal. Most chemical fertilizers release nutrients into the soil all at once, even if labeled "slow release."

Sometimes the release is too fast, so the plants can't absorb the nutrients efficiently, and some of the nutrients get washed away. These fertilizers can burn plants if they're applied incorrectly. Chemical fertilizers usually only provide nitrogen, phosphorus, and potassium. Few of them add other nutrients, and none of them contribute texture-improving elements to the soil.

Cover crops, also called green manure, are crops that are grown for a season and then tilled into the soil. They have deep roots, and their root action opens the soil up to increase the air in the soil. And as they decompose, they release nitrogen into the soil and *add* rather than deplete nutrients. Red clover or alfalfa, with roots that extend to 9 feet, grow well in Massachusetts. Cover crops tend to be used on empty vegetable or annual beds and then tilled in.

Compost, sometimes called black gold, is the perfect organic amendment. It's a tonic for the garden. Compost improves soil texture, the ability of the soil to retain moisture and nutrients, minerals and micronutrients. You can also fertilize your plants by dissolving the compost in water, a solution called compost tea. Mike Murray of Organic Soil Solutions in Woburn makes his own compost tea and shares details on his Web site: www.organicsoil solutions.com. The young company TerraCycle (www.terracycle .net) makes a compost tea from worm castings called Worm Poop Sustained-Release Plant Food, which is packaged in recycled soda bottles.

Other amendments. One of the best amendments is chopped leaves. When I worked at Blithewold Mansion, Gardens & Arboretum, we added shredded leaves, compost, and a slow-release organic amendment to the soil every year. The soil in the gardens was soft, dark, crumbly, and moist. You could almost hear the plants sighing. Another intriguing amendment is kitty litter. Barbara Emeneau, a retired Massachusetts certified arborist who gardens in Winchester, has very sandy soil and uses a clay kitty litter to improve her soil's water-holding capability.

The kinds of organic materials that you have in your garden will depend on what's been growing there previously, what's growing there now, and the climate. That's the beauty of it. If you put back into your garden that which is already in your garden, then you're giving your soil what it most needs.

How to Compost

There are various schools of thought about composting. They range from the philosophy that "compost happens" to red wiggler worm composting systems to intricate three-bin managed systems. The system you favor depends on how quickly you want your compost.

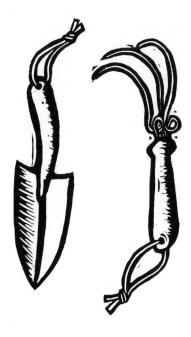

Simple piles work but you have to wait a while. You stack the material and let Mother Nature do the work. If you're in no hurry, then this is the simplest way to go—no work, no management, no fuss.

Worm bins using red wigglers (*Lumbricus rubellus*) can be set up in the house or garage. The worms eat kitchen scraps, and you collect their nutrient-rich castings to enrich the garden. These worms also multiply rapidly so you'll always have them and be able to give then away to friends. You can add red wigglers to your compost bin or pile outside.

The three-bin system requires forking the compost from one bin to the next to the next. It's actually a three-year system. You harvest the third year's compost for your garden as you tend to the second-year bin and add fresh material to the first-year bin.

Town Compost

Municipal composting sites are a source of compost, although you don't always know what you're getting. It's nice to be able to take your yard debris somewhere and know it's not going into a landfill. But when it comes to taking compost from the site, look for assurance that the pile has cooked well in case any diseased plants had been added to the pile. (I suggest you not use town compost on vegetable gardens just in case.)

Ecological landscape designer Ted Chapman says his city of Newton made 10,000 cubic yards of good quality compost in 2006. "The compost has been tested," he states, "and best of all it cost only $10 a cubic yard. We prepaid and picked it up in our own vehicle." To find a town compost site in your area, go to the Massachusetts Department of Environmental Protection's Bureau of Waste Prevention Web site: www.mass.gov/dep/recycle.

Good compost is a balance of "browns" and "greens" layered to ensure efficient decomposition and a good mix at the end. The browns are carbon-rich dry materials like straw, sawdust, dry grass clippings, and leaves. The greens are the nitrogen-rich materials like fresh grass clippings, eggshells, fresh manure, kitchen scraps, and human hair. It is possible to have bad compost—compost with diseased plants, weed seeds, or a bad mix of organic material won't be good for your garden. You can have your compost tested at the same place that tests your soil. Don't add dairy products and meats to your pile. It's not that they're actually bad for the compost, they just take longer to break down and can attract rodents and make your compost smell badly.

Good compost needs to be managed: aerated and moistened. If it's not composting properly, the mixture is probably too dry. If it smells it may be too wet.

Some composting enthusiasts are opposed to turning their piles, claiming that the disturbance inhibits the microbial activity. But Allen Barker, an authority on soil fertility and plant nutrition at the University of Massachusetts at Amherst, says the real goal of mixing materials is to aerate the pile. "Aeration of the pile provides oxygen to microorganisms that help to rot the organic matter," he says. "If the compost is not turned, it will become anaerobic and decomposition will be by fermentation." Fermentation processes are slower than the processes that occur in the presence of oxygen. "If you want compost in a relatively short period of time," says Barker, "you should turn the pile frequently." Otherwise it may take a year or two for the composting cycle to complete.

You say you don't have the space or patience to compost? You can buy composts and manures in bags at your local garden center. New lines of dehydrated composts are lightweight, easy to spread, and can be used as a mulch. Coast of Maine (www.coastofmaine .com) has an excellent product line. You can also order truckloads of compost from some garden centers that make their own. Mike Rocheleau at Homestead Organics in Boxborough creates a wonderful compost that he sells in bulk. He is passionate about his product and believes firmly that "incorporating compost into the soil is cost effective and results in significant benefits to plants and to the environment." Towns like Acton, he says, are urging home owners and contractors to incorporate more compost into lawns and landscapes as a way of conserving water. "Soils high in organic matter will retain much more water," adds Rocheleau, noting that a town with 5,000 residences each with 10,000 square feet of lawn could potentially save 94 million gallons of water as a result of increased organic matter in the soil.

Making compost is therapeutic. Your kitchen scraps feed your garden, the plants that didn't make it are reborn as compost (providing they were not sick or diseased), your leaves and grass clippings are put back to work. Nothing goes to waste, and you contribute to the cycle of life. What better way to create good soil and feel good at the same time?

The Site

Soil is only one element of a garden. You can improve your soil and even cheat your growing seasons a bit, but you can't fight the site. Wherever you live in Massachusetts, you need to learn to love your land—rocks, swamp, dunes 'n' all. Unless you have the money to truck in loads of perfect topsoil (or truck out loads of boulders), you have to accept the piece of earth you inherited and make of it a thing of beauty or a garden of plenty.

Know Your Zone

Temperatures directly affect what you can grow—and elevation influences temperatures. In Berkshire County, for instance, people garden at around 1,039 feet above sea level. This is distinctly different from Plymouth County, where the elevation ranges from sea level to only 400 feet at the summit of Manomet Hill. Elevation variations are one cause of temperature variation in the state. In general, for every 250 feet above sea level the temperature drops 1 degree Fahrenheit. The temperature in Pittsfield may be almost 10 degrees cooler than in Provincetown. That makes a huge difference in what survives the winter.

Here's where knowing your hardiness zone can be enormously helpful.

In 1960 the United States Department of Agriculture (USDA) mapped the country into areas, or zones, based on a 10-degree Fahrenheit difference in average annual minimum temperatures for each zone. These zones are called USDA Hardiness Zones and are used to identify which plants will survive low temperature. The zones range from Zone 1, with an annual minimum temperature of below 50 degrees, to Zone 10, with an annual minimum temperature of 35 to 40 degrees. The map was revised and updated in 1990 to include subzones, like 5a and 5b, and an additional Zone 11, which represents miminum temperatures above 40 degrees. The 1990 version of the USDA Hardiness Zone map is usually what appears in books. You can view this map online at the United States National Arboretum Web site: www.usna.usda.gov/Hardzone/ushzmap.html.

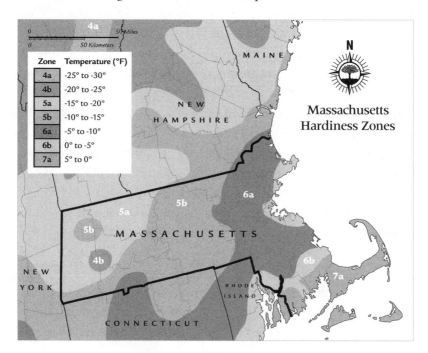

Zone	Temperature (°F)
4a	-25° to -30°
4b	-20° to -25°
5a	-15° to -20°
5b	-10° to -15°
6a	-5° to -10°
6b	0° to -5°
7a	5° to 0°

Massachusetts
Hardiness Zones

Hardiness zones are not a complete catalog of your area's growing conditions. But they are one of the best predictors of whether a plant will survive in your garden over the winter. The nursery and landscaping industry uses the information from the USDA map to label its plants with a hardiness zone or zones. Zone ratings are only a guide, not gospel. Knowing your USDA Hardiness Zone is useful when buying plants, but there are other factors involved in whether a plant lives or dies in your garden—microclimates, or pockets of warm or cold temperatures, being another key factor. So be aware of your zone, but don't rely solely on the hardiness zone designations.

Massachusetts Zones

In the Bay State the USDA Hardiness Zones range from 4b in the west to 7a in the east. No single county is just one zone! Hampshire County, for instance, is split almost vertically down the middle between Zones 5a and 5b, with blips of 6a in the southernmost part of the county. And Bristol County encompasses three zones: 6a, 6b, and 7a.

Here are the Massachusetts zones and what they mean in terms of the average annual minimum temperatures:

Zone 4b (–20°F to –25°F): Small area at intersection of Berkshire and Hampden Counties

Zone 5a (–15°F to –20°F): Berkshire, Franklin, some of Hampshire, and some of Hampden Counties

Zone 5b (–10°F to –15°F): Worcester, half of Hampshire and Hampden, and an area at the intersection of Franklin, Hampshire, and Berkshire Counties

Zone 6a (–5°F to –10°F): Essex, Middlesex, Suffolk, Norfolk, some of Bristol, a good chunk of Plymouth, and some of Hampden Counties

Zone 6b (0°F to –5°F): Boston, coastal areas north and south of Boston, and a swath across central Bristol and Plymouth Counties

Zone 7a (0°F to 5°F): Barnstable, Dukes, and Nantucket Counties

Frost Dates and Your Growing Season

Hardiness zone ratings predict which plants will survive your lowest temperatures, but the zones don't tell you when those low temperatures occur. Your "growing season" is defined as the number of days between the last frost of the spring and the first frost of the fall. Your growing season, or "frost-free days," will determine when to plant in the spring and when to cease garden cultivation in the fall.

Two USDA maps—the last spring frost map and the first autumn frost map—give general frost dates for the United States: The last frost in Massachusetts is estimated to occur from April 1 to April 30 and the first frost from November 1 to 30. You have to dig deeper to unearth the frost dates for your area. For freeze and frost data from locations around the state, check the University of Massachusetts Extension Web site at www.umassgreeninfo.org/fact_sheets/plant_culture/freeze_frost/_MA.pdf. Click on Climate Data. Additional information is available from the National Weather Service at www.nws.noaa.gov.

Below are some typical frost dates pulled from the National Oceanic and Atmospheric Administration Web site. Consider these dates to be general guidelines only. Readings posted on the site are commonly made at a height of 5 feet, and actual ground temperature can be 4 to 8 degrees less. Ground frost can occur even when the measured air temperature is 36 degrees. Site specifics, radiational cooling, air drainage, and other factors will influence actual frost dates at your location, the NOAA site says.

	Typical last frost (spring)	Typical first frost (fall)
East: Boston	May 3	November 8
Central: Worcester	May 7	October 2
West: Pittsfield	May 12	September 27

As you can see, frost dates vary greatly around the state, resulting in a different number of frost-free days and therefore different growing seasons. On Nantucket, John Bartlett of Bartlett's Farm says his growing season is safe from frost from Memorial Day to Columbus Day. "We plant our first seeds outside around April 20, and the last harvest date can be into November," he says. "The ocean keeps us warm in the fall but cool in the spring." On the other side of the state in Barre, the last frost date is usually June 1 but sometimes can be as late as June 15, according to Julie Rawson of Many Hands Organic Farm. And the first frost date of the year is usually by October 8, sometimes by September 20, and in a rare year as late as October 20. "One year it was August 23!" Rawson says.

The only way you can *really* know the frost dates in your exact location is to check with your local garden centers to see if they have kept records. Talk to your neighbors. Or start keeping your own records.

Types of Frost

We all know that frost occurs at 32 degrees Fahrenheit. But there are in fact three different categories of frost:

Light freeze: 32 to 36 degrees. Tender plants are killed, but not much harm is done to other plants.

Moderate or normal freeze: 28 to 32 degrees. This will destroy most annuals and cause particular damage to fruit blossoms and to tender and semihardy plants. It will also kill off the tops of perennials and may damage some shallow-rooted perennials.

Hard or severe freeze: 28 degrees. This will kill susceptible plants outright. At these temperatures the ground freezes solid, with the depth of the freeze dependent on the length of the freeze, soil moisture, and soil type.

Frost does not *have* to determine the beginning and end of your growing season. Folks who garden in the colder areas of Massachusetts may want to extend and protect their harvest. whereas the folks in eastern Massachusetts, where it's warmer, may only need to see the season out. Extending your growing season means holding on to the sun's warmth for as long as you can.

Do this by diligently protecting crops. Floating row covers, movable greenhouses, temporary hoop houses, cold frames, cloches, hot caps, and mulch are all devices to retain warmth so that plants can grow more quickly in spring and keep growing after autumn frost. Heavy mulching can help warm the soil in spring and retain heat and moisture in the fall. Shredded leaves, seaweed, and salt hay are great winter mulches. Just remember to lift the heavy mulch in the spring to help the soil warm up and get things moving in the garden. Lighten up on the mulch during the growing season.

Of course, you can defy the cold and grow plants year-round if you really want, but that requires a lot of effort and protection for your crops. Eliot

Coleman's *The Four Season Harvest* thoroughly details how to do this. Another marvelous book is *A Gardener's Guide to Frost: Outwit the Weather and Extend the Spring and Fall Seasons* by Philip Harnden.

The Specifics of Your Site

How well do you know your garden's weather and climate? "Weather" means atmospheric conditions like heat, cold, rain (or lack of), wind, and snow. "Climate" refers to those particular conditions that happen in a specific region. *Your* climate is the weather in your area, or even your garden. For instance, the humidity in Swampscott to the east and on the coast will differ greatly from the humidity in Springfield, which is further west and inland. Temperatures in a city garden will generally be several degrees warmer than those rural gardens in the hills because city buildings and streets retain heat. Leo Blanchette of Blanchette Gardens in Carlisle lives in a frost pocket, which means he is prone to early and late frosts. Barbara Dombrowski of Goose Cove Gardens in Gloucester contends with desiccating winds and damaging salt spray where she is close to the ocean.

Knowing your own property intimately is every bit as important as knowing what area of the state you live in and its general hardiness and heat zones. "The right plant in the right place" is the enduring mantra. Plants that adapt to your situation will be the easiest to grow. Different plants need different growing conditions: Vegetables love full sun all day, so a happy vegetable garden would be on a gentle slope facing south, with good water drainage, protected from the harsh winds but with just the right amount of airflow. Perennials can handle varied conditions. Some thrive in shade, partial shade, or full sun; others celebrate damp situations.

Before you plant your garden, assess your property's topographical features, orientation, sun exposure, wind exposure, airflow, microclimates, water drainage, existing plantings, views, and location of property lines and utilities.

Keep an open mind when assessing your site. What might look like a negative could turn out to be a positive—or at least made into one. Mashpee landscape designer Paul Miskovsky on the Cape took on a design project with a substantial site challenge: a half-acre kettle hole that encompassed most of the client's property. But Miskovsky transformed this land depression from a black hole of brambles and weeds into a treasure trove of artfully engineered swaths of plants, a water feature, gazebos, secluded spots for repose, and pathways and open spaces for the client's family to enjoy.

Topography

Is your property on a steep hill? Is it gently sloping or flat? Or is it a combination of hill and flatland? Is it on a rocky coast or in a valley? If you have hills, you may need to grade, build terraced beds, or landscape steps into the side of the hill to retain soil and water. If you have completely flat land, you may need help to ensure good drainage so that water doesn't pool and create soggy conditions inhospitable to plants you want to grow.

Topographical features include things like rivers, lakes, ponds, or swamps. You are a lucky gardener if you have a large body of water on your property—and not just for aesthetic reasons. Water takes longer to warm in the spring, but it retains warmth well into the fall. This warmth and humidity can benefit a nearby garden. If you have an overly damp garden, you may be able to construct a pond, water feature, or bog. There are plants for every situation.

Orientation

Track the sun through the day and through a year and record how the sun changes its angle and direction in your garden hour by hour and season by season. Locate south to orient vegetable beds for optimum sun exposure. You may want to create a shade garden on the north side of the house or a perennial bed on the east side that gets sun half the day. Again, there are plants for every situation.

Airflow and Wind

Air flows downhill the same way water flows downhill. If your garden is on the side of a hill, the air will flow through it, which is good. If your garden is at the top of the hill, the air may batter the plants. If it's at the bottom of the hill, your plants may "drown" in a pool of cold air. A breeze is a positive—a howling wind is not. Landscape architect David Bartsch on Nantucket often has to deal with winds of 50 miles per hour. "It can be a real challenge to garden under those conditions," he says. The sunken gardens in town, however, have their own protection against the wind and trap the sun's warmth.

Air needs to flow through a garden for the health of the plants but not so forcefully that it pounds them. Keep the air moving. You may need to divert the airflow by clearing a path and redirecting it by means of a built structure or strategically planted shrubs. Windbreaks need to be permeable so that air can flow through and should not be so high as to cut down on available sunshine. And just as you track the sun's seasonal movements, track the wind through the seasons. You may not need windbreaks year-round.

Microclimates

A microclimate is the weather and climate in a small pocket or area of your property or neighborhood. Even though the USDA Hardiness Zones map may place you in Zone 6b, you may have areas on your property that defy the zone for any number of reasons. It might be something as simple as your side of the street, as is the case with garden writer Fran Gustman in Brighton, who maintains that the opposite side of her street is "always at least two weeks ahead." Essentially her street has two microclimates.

Microclimates occur naturally or you can create them. You may have a completely exposed garden on a hillside subject to harsh winds. You had all but given up gardening there until you put in a windbreak of trees and shrubs. Or you may have a sun trap created by a wall of your house in conjunction with a nearby hedge. Here the plants are toasty warm and protected from the wind, even when the wind howls elsewhere through the garden. Crisse MacFadyen in Pittsfield grows tropical plants on a small patio that is completely protected from the elements, including the rain. Her patio traps the sun and retains the heat, creating a minitropics. Kath Holland, a Massachusetts Horticultural Society (MHS) master gardener in Easton, theoretically gardens in Zone 6a but finds that she is better off with plants hardy to Zone 5. Her one exception is a daphne (*Daphne caucasia*), which she keeps because the fragrance is hard to resist. She grows this finicky plant in a shady spot protected from the north-northwest wind by white pines. She defies the limitations of her hardiness zone by creating a microclimate in which her daphne is content.

You can exploit your site's microclimates to extend the sequence of bloom. Joann Vieira, director of horticulture at the Zone 5b Tower Hill Botanic Garden in Boylston, gives an example. "At the foundation of the farmhouse, tumbling over heat-retaining stone steps on the south side, we have planted a winter jasmine (*Jasminum nudiflorum*)," she says. "We also have it planted in the lawn garden, about 250 feet away, where it is a bit shaded, slightly lower in elevation, and on an east-facing slope. Last year in the cottage garden the jasmine began to bloom on March 29, whereas in the lawn garden it did not begin until April 25!"

Tim Boland, executive director of the Polly Hill Arboretum on Martha's Vineyard, notes that the USDA map places the arboretum in Zone 7a, "but in fact I would say we are in Zone 6b. I look at growing things outside a zone as challenging and fun, but climate and soil are always the limiting factors. You can create microclimates by using standard methods like buildings, built structures, walls, courtyards, windscreens, and so forth. While it is good to try to be a 'zone-buster,'" Boland says, "you will more often than not be disappointed. Use the zone map as a guide."

Water and Drainage

Use a rain gauge to track average precipitation in your garden. You can also get annual rainfall statistics from the National Weather Service at www.nsw.noaa.gov.

Note, too, how water behaves on your property. "Go out in your garden during a rain and watch how the water moves across your land," advises Jean Aker, landscape architect and professor at the Conway School of Landscape Design. "Low spots can be discerned much easier in the rain." She advises using these natural qualities to your advantage.

Existing Plantings

What you inherit on your land could be gorgeous—or not. Old foundation plantings may need to be ripped out to make way for new ones. You may have beautiful old shade trees or ugly trees that shade too much of the garden and need to be pruned or cut down.

The plants you inherit are indicators of what grows well in your garden. A friend of mine found native Solomon's seals (*Polygonatum biflorum*) and lady ferns (*Athyrium felix-femina*) on her property. These plants do well in dry woodland, which is what she has. She says that if she had really taken note of these existing plants, she wouldn't have tried—and failed—with woodland plants that need moister conditions.

Views

You may want to enhance naturally beautiful views to the ocean or block out an eyesore next door. Assess the lines of sight—the view from the house to the road, the view from the road to the house, the view out to your perennial bed or your vegetable garden or your pond. All these should be factored in when planning where to locate your beds and other plantings. Bear in mind that beautiful open views may herald problems with wind.

Property Lines and Utilities

An official surveyor's map will show your property demarcations and the location of your septic system, power, and utility lines. You don't want to plant your favorite specimen tree on someone else's property or right under a power line.

All in all, get to know your land and build a relationship with it. Enhancing existing positive conditions and minimizing the negative aspects of your property will go a long way toward creating a wonderful gardening experience for you, whatever your site.

Water

Water and how we use it is an important part of gardening. All plants need water to grow, but not all plants need the same amount of water. It's vital to know the water needs of your particular choice of plants. Selecting plants that can adapt to both your growing conditions and your watering practices is important, too. If you're not faithful about watering, then don't grow plants that need a constant supply of moisture!

The overall average rainfall for Massachusetts is 43 inches per year. But there are swaths and pockets around the state where this differs: To the west between the Deerfield and the Housic Rivers, the annual rainfall can be as much as 60 to 70 inches per year; the same is true for the Wachusett area. Your need for supplemental watering will be different if you live in the hills to the

Rain Data

You can find the data on precipitation in Massachusetts at a number of different Web sites:

- National Weather Service: www.nws.gov.
- Wunderground is a fun site with lots of climate data: www.wunderground.com.
- National Atlas of the United States of America: www.nationalatlas.gov. This site is particularly user friendly. Look under Climate and you'll be able to locate a map of Massachusetts with the precipitation clearly illustrated. You can then find your own town with its annual rainfall data.

west or the beach towns to the east, just as watering needs on the Cape will be a little different from watering requirements in Pittsfield.

Temperatures affect how much you need to water. They can differ as much as 15 degrees around the state. On the same day in late spring 2004, temperatures were, from east to west, 45 degrees in Provincetown, 57 degrees in Boston, 61 degrees in Worcester, and 54 degrees in Pittsfield. Warmer temperatures cause soil to dry more quickly than cooler temperatures.

Wind is drying. A garden on a hilltop in Worcester may dry as easily as a garden near a windy beach on Nantucket. The type of soil in your garden affects how much water you need. Clay soils tend to get waterlogged, and sandy soils tend to drain too well. Soil drainage translates to how well water is transmitted through the surface soil and subsoil, and most landscape plants, fruit trees, and berry bushes need good drainage to a depth of at least 2 feet. If your garden does not drain well and water pools, you may want to garden in raised beds. Creating drainage systems such as gravel pits or seepage pits are expensive alternatives.

How Much to Water

Disease and mineral deficiencies can exhibit similar-looking symptoms to those of overwatering or underwatering. If your plants are looking less than wonderful, do a little research before you throw water at them.

The goal in watering sensibly is to make sure your garden gets adequately watered without overwatering, underwatering, or wasting water. Plants absorb water by drawing it up through the plant and releasing it into the air—a process called *transpiration*. You need to know how much water each plant needs. A large tree may draw up to 400 gallons of water a day from the soil and release it into the atmosphere. Overwatering is both harmful to plants, wasteful, and expensive. Plants literally drown if there is too much water in the soil. Overwatering can cause root and fungal diseases, create a habitat for slugs and snails, and wash nutrients from the soil. Plants struggle to absorb nutrients from dry soil, so underwatering leads to smaller flowers and fruit, weaker plants, and dehydration.

Water long, deep, and infrequently. The rule of thumb is to give your garden 1 inch of water a week all at one time but slowly—about ½ inch an hour—so that the water has a chance to soak in. That 1 inch of water *should* wet the soil down to 12 inches, but check by digging down 1 foot with a trowel. It might take a long time to wet very dry soil. If you water for half an hour and then dig into the soil to find it's wet only to ½ inch deep, then you know your soil requires a longer watering session.

Infrequent but long and deep watering will encourage deep rooting. Frequent light watering encourages shallow rooting. Roots follow the water, and if water is on the surface only, then that's where the roots stay. Adjust water to the needs of the plant. Roses, for instance, may require as much as five to eight gallons a week. Some experts recommend watering for as much as two to three hours every two weeks, particularly for newly planted trees. Never allow seedlings to dry out because they probably won't recover.

Measure the amount of rainwater and sprinkler water received by your garden by placing a rain gauge into the soil or attaching it to a low post. Or sink a recycled plastic container into the garden. If your garden is on different levels, use different gauges throughout, because your garden may not be getting the same amount of water everywhere.

When the soil is truly wet, stop watering.

When to Water

Water when the plants need to be watered—not because the calendar says you should or simply because you haven't watered for

Rain Barrels

Drought conditions—and the ensuing water restrictions—are becoming increasingly common. Fortunately there are ways of "harvesting" what rain does fall and keeping it stored for use when it's not raining: rain barrels.

A rain barrel catches rainwater, which is naturally soft water with no chlorine, fluoride, minerals, and other chemicals. Rainwater is what plants like most. A rain barrel can be a plain old barrel or a fancy one made of plastic and equipped with mesh screens, brass spigots, bottom drains, and overflow valves. A rain barrel's capacity is usually sixty to eighty gallons. The best location for the barrel is under a roof downspout. If possible install the barrel at a height above where you want to water to give you some water pressure. If you have no pressure, you can either use this water in watering cans or install an inexpensive pump to get it moving.

Make sure your barrel has a cover to prevent debris from collecting, to prevent children or even pets from falling in, and to discourage mosquitoes. Some folks add a little fertilizer to the water in their barrels so they always have a supply of "high-octane" water for their plants. If you do that, make sure to keep the "octane" dilute so you don't overfertilize.

Harvesting rainwater is a great way to save money because you're not using municipal water. Finding rain barrels is easy. A great Web site that provides in-depth information about rain barrels with links to suppliers is www.rainbarrelguide.com. Sometimes master gardener associations will guide you to suppliers, or they may set up a bulk rain-barrel purchase system, so check in with them.

a while. Check the condition of your garden. Maybe the sun hasn't been shining or temperatures have been lower than normal and the garden hasn't dried out enough to need water. Many plants require less water once they are fully established. (This may take up to three years in the case of trees.)

The optimum time for watering is early morning, because that gives the plants many hours to absorb the water before temperatures rise and the water evaporates. The next best time to water is in late afternoon, when the leaves still have a chance to dry off before the cooler temperatures of the evening. If you leave the watering until evening, temperatures may drop while the garden is still wet and create damp conditions loved by diseases and slugs, snails, and other pests.

It is inefficient to water in the middle of the day when temperatures are at their highest. This is wasteful and there are no rewards for the plants. At best much of the water may simply evaporate, at worst the water beads act as magnifying lenses that burn the leaves. Garden professional Betsy Williams of the Proper Season in Andover has seen firsthand the damage wrought by midday watering: "I've had plants scorch and cook." Now, she says, "I usually water in the early morning or late afternoon, but never in the middle of the day during hot, dry times."

Having said all of that, it is better to water your plants when they need it, even if it's not the optimum time to do so, rather than not watering at all. We're all very busy and get to tasks when we can. Just be aware of the problems associated with watering at less than optimum times.

Water Wisely

The most efficient way to water is to apply it to the roots—that is, apply water directly to the soil and not onto the plants. That way water will arrive exactly where it is needed—the roots—and will not linger on the foliage and encourage disease.

- Roots of annuals are typically in the top 12 inches of soil.
- The root system of trees and shrubs may go down a couple of feet and extend two to five times the spread of the branches, but the feeder roots are close to the surface if not actually on the surface.
- Root systems of lawns are typically only 4 to 6 inches deep.

Use a watering system that directs water to the roots most efficiently. You don't want to spray your asphalt driveway, deck, pathways, house. . . . Fortunately you can choose from many effective watering systems.

Hand Watering

Watering with a watering can or a hose can be therapeutic. It gets you in touch with your garden so you can check how things are growing and look for prob-

lems. But to deeply hand water any portion of your garden would mean standing there for a long time. Better to keep your hand watering for containers and small beds. If you like to hand water, one method you can use is to sink perforated containers (clay or plastic) into the soil next to a plant. Fill the container and it will distribute water directly to the root system. This is particularly good if you notice one or two plants that are looking a little droopy. You don't water everything just because of the needs of a few.

Sprinklers

There are many types of sprinklers: overhead, stationary, pulsating or impulse, rotary, and oscillating. Some sprinklers are hard to adjust for range or direction, and you'll find yourself watering areas that don't need it—the neighbor's yard, your car in the driveway. . . . Any sprinkler that keeps the water close to the ground is more efficient because there's less chance for evaporation. Some sprinklers are better for different areas of the garden.

Michael Carter gardens with his partner, Roger Dextradeur, on twenty-one acres in Swansea. He has an elaborate sprinkler system that he created with hoses hidden underground: "I have over fifty of them throughout the garden," he says. "We have sprinklers with manual shutoffs." The two also created a pond 100 by 135 feet and nearly 12 feet deep, from which they harvest irrigation water during the dry season.

Overhead sprinklers spray water high overhead. I particularly like noodle-head sprinklers because I can direct the spray exactly where I want it for each different area. The disadvantage of overheads is that some water will evaporate before it reaches the ground.

Impulse or pulsating sprinklers operate on lower water pressure yet can discharge more water over a greater area than other sprinklers. You adjust the spray to reach only the target area, which is a more efficient use of water. You control the height of the stream to allow sprinkling under low tree branches and adjust the stream from full jet to fine mist. The spray is strong and close to the ground, so it is wind resistant.

Automatic sprinkler systems have one big disadvantage: They're automatic. Sure, you don't have to be around to switch them on and off, but people don't always take the time to override the automatic features when plants don't need water. As the seasons change so too do the moisture requirements of plants, and the sprinkler system should be reprogrammed. It's important to install a rain shutoff device for automatic systems. Automatic systems can be complicated to program, and they require maintenance. Part of the system may stop working and you'll have uneven watering—and you may not even notice until part of your lawn or garden dies.

Soaker Hoses

Soaker hoses "sweat" water along their entire length. They are made of a porous material that allows water to soak or weep through directly to the soil. Lay out your soaker hoses by winding them through the beds, spacing them to get as close to plants as possible to treat plants evenly.

Water pressure may be a factor with soaker hoses. Don't make the hoses so long that water can't make it to the end—otherwise plants far from the faucet get shortchanged. By using a Y connector at the faucet, you can have several shorter hoses watering at the same time. As with any watering system, check to make sure it's operating correctly. Dig into soil one hour after watering to check soil moisture depth.

Drip Irrigation

Drip irrigation gets water directly to the soil through tiny outlets called emitters. As with soaker hoses, the drip irrigation hose is laid on the ground between plants or is installed under the soil.

When to Water

You know it's time to water when . . .

- Soil is dry below the surface.
- Wilted leaves on trees and shrubs will not perk up in the evening.
- Leaves on trees turn yellow and drop before the fall.
- Lawns are a dull green and footprints show.
- It's difficult to push a screwdriver or trowel into the soil.

It's easier to detect a problem when the hoses are above ground, but the hoses are not attractive and may look better covered with mulch or leaves. The hoses are placed around individual plants or spaced to soak entire beds in areas that are densely planted. It is easier to match plant needs and soil types with a drip system, particularly in large or sloped areas where water pressure may make soaker-hose output erratic.

Intelligent Irrigation

If you have plenty of rainfall and are in no danger of going without water, then you are a lucky gardener. Most of us experience periods of drought during the summer and must conserve water and irrigate intelligently. Remember, whether you are using municipal water or water from a well, it's coming from the same place—groundwater reservoirs. During town water bans, some folks think it's fine to post a sign on their lawn saying IT'S OKAY, WE'RE USING WELL WATER and then run their sprinkler systems. Using well water is still depleting the same water supply, so maybe it's not so fine.

Your irrigation system can be informal—you and the watering can when needed—or you can get very sophisticated with a combination of sprinklers, soaker hoses, and supplemental hand watering. As you make your irrigation plan, consider these approaches:

Build irrigation zones into your design. This means grouping plants with similar water needs together. Choose plants that need minimal water, and remember that many plants require less water once they are established—that is, after two or three years.

Prioritize what needs to be watered. You may want to place young plants that need extra coddling at the top of your list, or plants that matter the most to you, or simply the ones that really need more water.

Mulch to conserve water. "Where I live in Boston, I mulch,

mulch, mulch. A 2- to 4-inch layer of organic mulch will conserve water and reduce weeds," says Sally Williams, editor of the *Garden Literature Index*. She says compost is the best mulch because it adds nutrients to the soil, unlike bark chips that can reduce some nutrients, and unlike stone mulch that adds no nutrients. Buckwheat hulls are a favorite mulch because they allow water to pass through without absorbing any of the water. "Keep mulch from touching plant stems," she advises. "When mulching around trees, I leave a gap of a few inches between tree trunk and mulch to discourage rodents, insects, and disease."

Gardeners who mulch may still need to water—just less frequently. Daniel Botkin farms organically at Laughing Dog Farm in Gil and says he's been lucky with fortuitous rains three of the last four years. But he knows he could be caught dead by severe drought since the farm's soil is well drained and entirely exposed on a hilltop. "We use massive quantities of mulch hay and still need to irrigate and aerial water in critical spots," he says.

Minimize runoff. Create berms around plants to contain water. Carefully water sloped areas to ensure the plants are actually getting watered. You may want to terrace so that water stays put, or build diversions so that you can harvest runoff. Channel water in the garden by creating swales, which are indentations built into the garden almost like a shallow furrow. Divert roof runoff to spread over well-drained soil. Use porous paving materials on driveways and walkways so that runoff is reabsorbed back into the groundwater supply.

Plant in trenches and bowls. Frank Albani Jr. farms at Golden Rule Farm in Plymouth and is president of the Massachusetts chapter of the Northeast Organic Farmers Association (NOFA/Mass). To make the very best use of water, he recommends that you plant in trenches for rows and bowls for individual plants. "I build soil ridges to hold water right in the root zone," he says. "Using a hose or watering can, I flood the root zones. I'm only watering the vegetables and not the weeds in between."

Improve soils with amendments, says Ed Stockman, organic extension educator for NOFA/Mass. "Conditioning soil can greatly enhance soil productivity and its ability to absorb and hold water." He advises building a garden soil with a high percentage of organic matter. "This is the best way of initiating a program of water conservation. The greater the organic matter, the more water a soil can hold. Soils with high organic content need to be irrigated less even under hot, dry conditions." A soil with high

Water-Wise Tips

- Dig to loosen the soil and encourage water absorption. Try not to dig in dry weather because the soil dries out fast.
- Weeds compete for water and nutrients. Keep up with the weeding.
- Shelter plants from drying winds, and shade seedlings.
- Use gray water wherever possible. This is recycled household water from your shower, rinsed dishes, or any previous use of water that does not leave the water contaminated with bacteria or detergents.

organic-matter content, explains Stockman, has a texture with increased porosity, which allows rain and irrigation to enter the soil easily rather than run off. "Once water has entered the soil, the organic matter is willing and able to capture this water and store it for the future needs of both the crop and soil biota."

Xeriscaping in Massachusetts

Xeriscaping is the term used for landscaping with indigenous and drought-tolerant plants that, once established, are particularly adapted to going without much water. Xeric plants are happy in your dry garden. Xeriscaping is also a way of conserving water. Soil expert Normand Helie in Cherry Valley has specific recommendations for gardening in dry conditions:

1. Select plants carefully to ensure the right plants for your conditions.
2. During the plant establishment period, water may be necessary because roots are few and only inside the container or rootball. Once roots enter the soil on the site, it is best to leave them alone by cutting back on water to promote good genetic material that will tolerate dry conditions.
3. Plant large screenings to prevent plants drying out from driving winds.
4. Use antitranspirant sprays when water tables are low and plants are undergoing severe moisture stress.
5. Allow drying cycles to occur to build xeric characteristics in the plant. Don't interfere with proper growth. Everything you do influences the growth of a xeric plant, so don't water it during dry times.
6. Let the weak die and replace them with new plants until the site becomes established with carefree species.
7. Be sure the plants are properly nourished, especially with potassium, to optimize water conservation within the plant.
8. And, of course, mulch.

A xeric garden isn't going to look like a lush English cottage garden. "Don't have high expectation of what this area should look like," Helie says. "Expect some drying and desiccation. Don't pamper the area, otherwise it will never build the character qualities that the plants genetically have."

Drought-Tolerant Plants

What are good xeric plants for Massachusetts? Barbara Emeneau, a retired Massachusetts certified arborist and longtime gardener in Winchester, recommends these trees and shrubs:

Viburnum (*Viburnum* x *bodnantense*). A deciduous shrub with beautiful pink flowers and dark green leaves.

American smoke tree (*Cotinus obovatus*). A small tree with gray to gray brown bark. Leaves turn brilliant orange red, and pinkish gray panicles give the plant its smokey look.

Cornelian cherry (*Cornus mas*). A shrub or small tree with leaves that turn red purple in fall. It produces yellow flowers in spring.

Japanese pagoda tree (*Sophora japonica*). A deciduous tree covered in small creamy white flowers in summer.

Creeping myrtle (*Vinca minor*). An evergreen sub-shrub with white flowers.

For Dan Botkin in Gil, the vining crops seem to be the winners for dry areas: "Melons and squash can be effectively grown through droughty conditions so long as their hill or mound is insulated from drying out," he says.

Michael Carter in Swansea uses a lot of ornamental grasses. "These seem to tolerate the lack of moisture," he says.

Award-winning landscape designer Paul Miskovsky in Mashpee has his own list of drought-tolerant winners:

Upright English oak (*Quercus robur fastigiata*). Big, upright, with textured bark and dark green leaves.

Japanese black pine (*Pinus thumbergii*). A lovely conical tree with dark gray green leaves.

Northern bayberry (*Myrica pensylvanica).* A deciduous to semievergreen large shrub with dark green leaves and yellow catkins in spring.

Lavender (*Lavandula angustifolia*) 'Hidcote' and 'Munstead'. 'Hidcote' lavender is compact, with dark purple flowers; 'Munstead' flowers are blue purple.

Stonecrop 'Autumn Joy' (*Sedum* 'Herbstfreude'). This comes into its own in fall, with rusty red flowers on greenish gray stems.

Daylily 'Happy Returns' (*Hemerocallis* spp.). Keeps on blooming with light yellow flowers.

Shasta daisy 'Alaska' (*Leucanthemum* x *superbum*). A daisy-like white flower that never seems to stop blooming.

Switch grass (*Panicum virgatum* 'Heavy Metal'). Stiff, metallic, blue gray blades turn yellow in the fall.

Cape American beach grass (*Ammophila breviligulata*). Used to stabilize beach dunes, this tough, erect grass looks wonderful in a beach-type garden.

Landscape gardener Mary Shane of Mary Shane, Inc. in Marlborough has a favorite drought-tolerant landscape element and it isn't a plant—"it's a boulder!" She systematically incorporates fieldstone into her designs, especially in gardens where watering is an issue because "the client won't water or there isn't any watering source except rain," she says. She uses hens and chicks and other low-growing sedums around the boulders because they do well with little water once established.

Plants with Wet Feet

For the folks who get abundant rainfall, particularly those in central Massachusetts, here are plants that prefer to have wet feet, recommended by Saugus-based landscape designer and lecturer Laura Eisener, who is also the Massachusetts editor of *People, Places & Plants*.

Red maple (*Acer rubrum*). "A classic!" she says. It turns bright red in fall.

Winterberry (*Ilex verticillata*). A shrub or small tree with white flowers in spring, followed by dark red or scarlet fruit.

Spicebush (*Lindera benzoin*). A deciduous shrub with bright green leaves that turn yellow in fall. It has lovely yellowish flowers in spring.

Buttonbush (*Cephalanthus occidentalis*). This shrub can reach to 20 feet but usually stays smaller. The new branch growth is green or red, while older growth is brown; the leaves are glossy dark green.

Highbush blueberry (*Vaccinium corymbosum*). An upright deciduous shrub with pinkish flowers in spring and leaves that turn yellow or red in fall.

Cardinal flower (*Lobelia cardinalis*). A clump-forming perennial with bright green leaves and scarlet red flowers.

Marsh marigold (*Caltha palustris*). This aquatic perennial has dark green leaves and yellow waxy flowers and can grow in water.

I find watering my garden calming. I know I'm doing something good for my plants, and I love to see water droplets sparkling on the leaves of my lady's mantle or European ginger. I can stand for the longest time with a hose, watching the hummingbirds dart in and out of the spray. It's magic.

Green Things

CHAPTER FOUR

Annuals

Annuals send me into a frenzy of delight: small mounded flowers, tall willowy flowers, plants that love the sun and those that savor shade, plants with great foliage, plants that trail, plants that climb, and more. And such great names! Love-in-a-mist (*Nigella*), Queen Anne's thimble (*Gilia*), or golden goddess (*Bidens*). I love the ease and speed with which annuals grow and their continuing abundance of flowers. Massachusetts gardeners can use annuals in so many ways: as cut flowers, among vegetables, in beds devoted to them, in a perennial bed, in containers, climbing up tepees, or sprawling over walls. In one season they come and they go, so next year you can try something different or replant your favorites. You don't have to worry about overwintering these plants through a finicky New England winter.

An annual germinates, grows to maturity, sets seed, and dies all in one season. In general, annuals are categorized as hardy, half-hardy, or tender.

Hardy annuals are what they say—tough and hardy. Sow them before the last frost, as soon as the ground can be worked. You can start them indoors a few weeks before the last frost date for earlier bloom. Some can be sown outdoors in fall for spring germination. English marigold (*Calendula officinalis*) or mallow (*Lavatera trimestris*) are designated hardy. Hardy annuals are often confused with biennials.

Half-hardy annuals are more sensitive to cold than hardy annuals. They can be started indoors six to eight weeks before the last frost date and set out after the last frost, although they can take a slight frost if your timing isn't perfect. Blanketflower (*Gaillardia*) and gazania are examples of half-hardy annuals.

Tender annuals need TLC. They don't tolerate any cold and will be killed by frost. Start them indoors about ten weeks before the last frost date. Don't put them out until two to three weeks *after* the last frost. In fact, don't plant them until the soil is warm. Impatiens is a tender annual, as is rose moss (*Portulaca grandiflora*).

Some of the plants that we treat as tender annuals in the Bay State are actually biennials and perennials in other regions. They simply cannot survive the harsher New England winters. Coleus, impatiens, and some salvias are examples of these plants, which are also known as "tender perennials." Many Massachusetts gardeners use them in their designs as if they were annuals.

Choosing Annuals

When people think of annuals, they usually think of plants that love full sun. Not many annuals like the shade—they may survive in the shade but will probably become weak and leggy. A few that can handle the shade include gomphrena (*Gomphrena globosa*) and pincushion flower (*Scabiosa atropurpurea*).

Your choices of annuals are many and varied, and most are easy to grow. Some annuals prefer to be sown directly outside, like coreopsis; others need to be started indoors, like petunias. Some annuals germinate in fewer than ten days, such as ageratum, while others need up to twenty-five days, like Transvaal daisy (*Gerbera lamesonii*).

New Annuals for New England Gardens

These twelve annuals were chosen by Tim Kane of Pride's Corner in Connecticut and featured in the spring 2006 issue of *People, Places & Plants* magazine.

- *Zinnia* 'Zowie Yellow Flame'. Scarlet rose center and yellow petal edges; sun.
- *Phlox* 'Intensia Cabernet'. Dark burgundy wine flowers; full sun to partial shade.
- 'Black Pearl' ornamental pepper. Full sun. All-America Selection winner.
- 'Blazin' Rose' iresine. Mix of bright rose, pink, and dark red; partial sun.
- *Lobelia* 'Laguna White'. Pure white flowers; partial shade.
- *Euphorbia* 'Diamond Frost'. Delicate small white blooms; sun or partial shade.
- *Impatiens* Fanfare 'Pink Sparkle'. Spreading impatiens. Large showy blooms, heat tolerant; full to partial shade.
- *Oxalis* 'Charmed' series. White to lavender, emerald green, violet; full to partial shade.
- *Helenium* 'Dakota Gold'. North American native, yellow; sun.
- 'Supertunia Vista Bubblegum'. Pink; full sun to partial shade. A 2006 Proven Winner.
- *Angelonia* 'Angelface Dresden Blue'. Soft lavender blue; full sun.
- *Sutera (Bacopa)* 'Cabana Trailing Blue'. Dark blue living carpet; full sun to partial shade.

The great thing about annuals is you're never stuck with a plant you don't like. You can choose different varieties every year. You've probably noticed that in recent years nurseries have started selling branded selections. Proven Winners and Blooms of Bressingham are just two of the branded selections of plants. Just remember that some branding is marketing, not a completely impartial assessment of plants.

In contrast, All-America Selections (www.all-americaselec tions.org) is a nonprofit organization that *does* evaluate plants impartially. AAS has a network of trial gardens throughout North America where flower and vegetable varieties are grown and assessed. The 2006 winners included *Dianthus* 'Supra Purple', *Nicotiana* 'Perfume Deep Purple', *Diascia* 'Diamonte Coral Rose', and *Viola* 'Skippy LX Red-Gold'. You can visit All-America

Tropicals as Annuals

Michel Marcellot of Seven Arrows Farm in Attleboro uses tropical plants as annuals. "I love to plant tropicals in the garden as soon as all threat of frost has passed," he says. "Tropical ferns, tender bamboos . . . you get the idea. Just because it won't survive the winter here is no reason not to enjoy it as long as it lasts!" Some of his favorites:

- Japanese aralia (*Fatsia japonica*)
- Elephant ear and taro (*Alocasia* and *Colocasia*)
- Bird of paradise (*Strelitzia reginae*)
- Thorn apple (*Datura*)
- Angel's trumpet (*Brugmansia*)
- Algerian ivy (*Hedera algeriensis*)
- Purphiok (*Tupistra chinensis*)
- Echevarias
- Agave

Selections display gardens at the Massachusetts Horticultural Society's Elm Bank gardens in Wellesley, the Berkshire Botanical Garden in Stockbridge, and the University of Massachusetts Amherst's Durfee Conservatory (see chapter 12).

Right Annual, Right Place

While it can be great fun to buy an armload of annuals on a whim, it can be a strain on your wallet. It is perhaps more satisfying to know what you want and why before you make your purchase. Have a design plan in mind. Are you using the annuals

for containers, to fill in spaces in a perennial bed, or for a cutting garden? Is your soil heavy clay as in Lenox or sandy loam like that on Nantucket? Some annuals, like the heavy-blooming hybrids, want fairly rich, fertile soil, whereas others, like nasturtiums, prefer poor soil. Do your research! In general, I find that as long as the soil has plenty of organic matter and a pH of 6 to 7, then I'll have success. "Annuals that do better in poor soils seem to do better on the Cape," says Mike Mahoney of Mahoney's Garden Centers. These include plants such as begonias, salvias, portulaca, brachyscome, and verbenas.

Climate is something of a factor when selecting annuals. For instance, the Cape has always done well with cold-tolerant annuals, adds Mahoney. "The cool winds on the Cape keep temperatures about 10 degrees cooler in summer, allowing things like

Annuals for Southern Massachusetts

Kathy Tracey of Avant Gardens in North Dartmouth shares some of her favorite annuals:

- Fame flower (*Talinum paniculatum* 'Kingswood Gold'). Golden foliage and sprays of pink flowers.

- Flowering tobacco (*Nicotiana langsdorfii*), with bell-shaped green blooms, and *N. mutabilis*, with blooms that start as white and fade to pink.

- Bush violet (*Browallia americana*). A garden filler with deep blue flowers and a white eye.

- *Salvia guaranitica* 'Black and Blue'. A tender perennial with cobalt blue flowers accented by black calyces.

- *Salvia* 'Indigo Spires'. Gorgeous blue flowers on tall, sturdy stems.

- Million bells (*Calibrachoa*). An ever-blooming substitute for petunia.

- Mexican bachelor button (*Centratherum*). Pretty dark lavender blue flowers.

- Cigar plant (*Cuphea* 'David Verity'). Long bloom period, easy care.

- *Fuchsia* 'Gartenmeister'. Orange salmon flowers and great foliage.

- Oregano (*Origanum rotundifolium* 'Kent Beauty'). A great container plant.

- Coleus. You can't beat the easy care and the selection of coleus foliage colors.

pansies to bloom longer. I remember older varieties of osteospermum would never go out of bloom on the Cape, but they would stop blooming up north around late June or early July." New heat-tolerant hybrids—such as Supertunias, Surfinas, verbenas, diascias, and alyssum—extend the bloomtime of plants that once petered out in the heat of inland portions of the state.

Selecting Plants at the Nursery

Your neighborhood garden center stocks plants that perform well locally. "What sells is what grows," says Mike Mahoney. "People see friends or neighbors have good luck with something, and through word of mouth pockets of trendy annuals pop up."

When you're in the garden center, don't be put off if plants are not in bloom. This probably means that the nursery has been diligent about pinching back to help the plants grow stronger roots and bush out. If they are in bloom, pinch off the flowers when you get the plants home, and you'll get many more blooms later, once the plant settles in. Avoid plants that look sickly— yellowed or spotted leaves or wilted, weak stems. Knock the plant gently out of its pot to check that the root system is healthy. The roots should be white, moist, and well distributed in the pot— circling roots mean the plant is pot bound. If you're not happy with the roots, don't buy the plant. An annual will be around only for one season. There's no point in bringing home a plant that needs months of coddling before it looks good.

Starting from Seed

Whether you sow seeds indoors or outside, your seed-starting date is determined by your area's last frost date. Working back from the last frost, calculate the number of weeks for seed germination and for the seedling to be strong and healthy enough to be planted outside. Take into consideration whether the plant is a hardy annual, half-hardy annual, or tender annual/tender perennial.

Seed annuals in flats or individual pots in a good soilless seed-starting mix. If you want to make your own mix, use equal parts peat moss, perlite, and vermiculite. The mix should be thoroughly moistened but not soggy. You can use dampened peat pots, too. *Park's Success with Seeds* by Anne Reilly is a must-have book if you like growing plants from seed.

Read the seed packet for germination instructions. Most seeds are sown at a depth equal to three times their diameter. Some seeds need darkness to germinate: Once the seeds are sown, cover the flats with a light-blocking material or put the flats in a warm, dark cupboard. Other seeds need light to germinate: Don't cover the seeds with the mix, just press the seeds in.

Most seeds need a growing condition that is moist and warm, so cover the flats with a plastic lid that holds in moisture and acts like a mini-greenhouse. I put my flats on top of the refrigerator in the basement. Lift the lid regularly to check the seeds; vent the lid if the soil is too moist and remove the cover when plants sprout.

You need a good source of light to grow annuals indoors—a *very* sunny windowsill can work if you turn the flats every day. A fluorescent light setup is more reliable. Leave the lights on for twelve to eighteen hours a day. (You can buy a timer for this purpose.) Place the lights 6 to 12 inches above the seedlings and lift the lights as the plants grow. Water to keep the soil moist, not wet. Bottom watering is effective because it doesn't disturb the seedlings.

If seedlings suffer from damping-off (a fungal disease that causes young

plants to wilt or collapse), you may lose some but not necessarily all the plants. Damping-off travels quickly, but I saved a flat of basil by taking a clean knife and cutting out more than the affected seedlings and throwing the chunk away. I managed to stop the spread of the disease and thus retained a good basil crop.

Seedlings with their second set of true leaves can be transplanted into individual pots. I prefer peat pots because the entire pot can be planted and the pots decompose. Some plants, like nasturtium and sweet peas, don't like to be disturbed or transplanted from a pot, so either plant the seed directly in the ground or in peat pots. When seedlings have four true leaves, you can spray them with a dilute liquid seaweed fertilizer.

Planting and Tending

Plants that have been grown indoors will need to go through the process of "hardening off" to prepare them for life outdoors. Put young plants outside for an hour the first day. Increase the amount of time each day until they've been outside all day and night. Then they can be planted. You can also harden off plants in a cold frame—control the temperature by lifting and closing the lids so the plants don't cook or freeze inside the cold frame.

The roots of annuals usually stay within the top 4 to 6 inches of soil. There are two schools of thought about preparing the soil for annuals. One school says dig deep and amend the soil with plenty of organic material because it will retain moisture and cause roots to grow deeper. The other school says deep cultivation isn't necessary because annuals' roots are shallow and tilling soil deeply exposes lots of weed seeds. The latter tends to be my approach. Annuals like cosmos and nasturtium prefer fairly poor or "lean" soil.

If some of your annuals have grown a bit leggy in the pot, you may be able to plant them deeply—to the depths of their lowest leaves. Plants that have adventitious roots (roots that grow out from the stem) can be planted deeper than normal. Sunflowers can be planted this way, as can tomatoes.

Annuals need basic care once in the ground. Mulch to keep weeds at bay and retain moisture, water (preferably with soaker hoses), remove weeds before they go to seed, and spot fertilize with a liquid seaweed fertilizer if you see some plants struggling. While most annuals need a richer soil because they will only be producing blooms for one season, others (like nasturtium) actually prefer a lean soil. Read the literature to find out what each annual needs. For the heavier feeders it is important to ensure they have all the nutrients they require. Slow-release fertilizers are a good addition to an annual planting.

Most annuals do better with regular deadheading. If an annual puts energy into setting seed, that's wasted energy. And some annuals will stop flowering once they develop seedpods. Pinching or cutting spent blooms not only stimulates the plant to put energy into new blooms but also makes it look nicer.

Vines

I have to make a plug for annual vines. They get overlooked but are such a pleasure to grow. Quickly sprouting up tepees, sprawling across fences, climbing up walls and over archways, they create a delightful effect in the garden. Black-eyed Susan vine (*Thumbergia alata*), cardinal climber (*Ipmoea* x *multifida*), hyacinth bean (*Dolichos lablab*), sweet peas (*Lathyrus odoratus*), and starglory (*Mina lobata*) are satisfying additions to the garden. The shocking pink Brazilian jasmine (*Mandevilla*) is one of my favorites. A perennial in its native Brazil, it grows quickly and works well as an annual in Massachusetts. If you feel inclined, you can cut it back and overwinter it in a greenhouse.

Containers

Annuals in containers give almost instant gratification. You can plant more closely than you would in a border. Since the plants will be in the container only for one season and use up only a 4- to 6-inch depth of soil, they will survive happily in close quarters. You can design and start your entire container indoors and put it outside when the weather is right. Just remember to harden off plants before doing so. You can also change plants easily as the seasons change.

At the End of the Season

As first frost approaches, you can harvest and save seeds. Collecting seeds is enormously satisfying and great for the wallet. Harvest the seed when ripe, usually when the seedpod or capsule turns brown and dry. Cut the capsule off at its base and let it fall into a paper bag or envelope. Store the bag indoors through the winter in a cool, dry place. Label the bag with the plant name and the year the seed was collected. Most seeds are viable for two to five years.

Many annuals cheerfully reseed themselves, thus earning the name self-sowers. Love-in-a-mist, for instance, will pop up everywhere in your garden, as will many annual poppies. This is great if you have a cottage-garden design. In a controlled design you may want to limit the number of self-sowers you introduce, or you will live with volunteers for a long time. I love it when I come across a *Nicotiana* or *Verbena bonariensis* in a surprising place. If I dislike it there, I remove it.

After frost there are two ways of handling annuals: Pull out the dead plants or leave their roots in the ground. Pulling out the annuals leaves holes in the beds that can look unattractive and serve as homes for weed seeds unless you top-dress with compost or mulch with shredded leaves. Lift much of this mulch in the spring to help the soil warm up. If you leave the plants in the ground, their root systems will decompose over the winter. Cut the plants back to the ground so the garden looks neater.

Either way, clear away debris that could potentially harbor insects, pests, or diseases. Since annuals are only around for one season, there's not much time for them to become disease ridden, but some varieties can be susceptible to powdery mildew, rust, and gray mold. Bag and trash the leaves and stems of infected plants to avoid a repeat performance next year. Removing debris also makes it more difficult for insects such as aphids, leafminers, spider mites, and whiteflies to overwinter. (Turn to chapter 10 for information on pests and diseases and how to control them.)

Growing and using annuals is a blast. Nothing beats wandering around the garden just before dinner doing a little stress-releasing deadheading or gathering flowers to go on the table. You can pick as many flowers as you'd like, because cutting them only encourages more flowers. The constant supply of blooms and the speed with which annuals grow make them great fun.

CHAPTER FIVE

Perennials

For some reason the term "perennial" conjures up the image of easy gardening. Just because a perennial, once established, can survive for five or more years does not mean that it survives in solitary without help!

Gardeners in Massachusetts deal with a wild variety of weather patterns every year, which makes getting our plants to perform the way we want a real challenge. Some years spring warmth arrives in April. Other years we experience true spring-like weather for only two weeks in May, followed immediately by hot summer temperatures and dry spells. What's a gardener to do? Select the right perennials, put them in the right place, and give them the care they need. This chapter explains how.

First, some definitions. A perennial is a plant that comes back year after year. It produces flowers and seeds more than once in its life span. When people think of perennials, what usually comes to mind are the standard herbaceous perennials like astilbe, monarda, daylily, and iris. But perennials also include cacti, succulents, wildflowers, ferns, grasses, bamboos, and roses.

Perennials can be herbaceous or woody.

Herbaceous perennials are those with soft stems. The top—stems, leaves, and flowers—usually dies to the ground each fall. The parts of the plant that are underground survive the winter. Bleeding heart (*Dicentra*) is a herbaceous perennial.

Woody perennials are often referred to as subshrubs. Their stems are woody and stiff. A woody perennial does not die back

Roses

In my view roses are in a category all their own. They are closer in habit to a woody perennial. I love roses, but I can't do them justice in the space of this book. I suggest contacting the American Rose Society at www.ars.org (their book, *The Rose*, is a helpful guide) and the Worcester-based New England Rose Society at www.rosepetals.org for rose-growing information specific to our region.

Stanley Park in Westfield (www.stanleypark.org) has received the All-America Rose Selections Outstanding Public Rose Garden Award, thanks in part to its more than fifty varieties of roses and 2,500 rosebushes. The peak season is mid-June through September. Another wonderful resource is Roseland (www.roselandroses.com), a family-owned nursery in Acushnet with an excellent reputation.

For books I recommend *Roses: A Care Manual* by Amanda Beales, although not all the roses mentioned are hardy in Massachusetts. Keep your ear to the ground for a new book by Mike and Angelina Chute, both American Rose Society certified consulting rosarians. Their book will focus exclusively on roses for New England.

to its crown or roots as does a herbaceous perennial, and so it generally is not cut back in fall. Woody perennials like Russian sage (*Perovskia*) are often pruned like a shrub.

Hardiness Zones and Perennials

Hardiness zone ratings are important when selecting perennials. Perennials fall into three categories based on their reaction to the cold.

Hardy perennials can survive Massachusetts winters without protection, or with very little protection.

Half-hardy or semihardy perennials need some protection (such as mulch) from winter cold.

Tender perennials, which are often tubers, bulbs, or rhizomes, won't survive the Massachusetts winters. They need to be lifted in fall, stored through the winter, and replanted the following spring when the soil warms. (Using tender perennials as annuals is discussed in chapter 4.)

Hardy perennials such as bellflower (*Campanula*), coneflower (*Echinacea*), and columbine (*Aquilegia*) can handle colder temperatures and therefore are rated for a different hardiness zone than tender perennials like a lot of the salvias, dahlias, or coleus. Remember, however, that your USDA Hardiness Zone rating (see chapter 2) is only a guideline. There is never a guarantee that a plant will survive in your garden, even if the experts say it will. Wayne Mezitt, chairman of Weston Nurseries in Hopkinton, feels that as a rule catalogs publish too liberal a climate zone for most plants. Jacqueline Cowles of Andrew's Greenhouse in Amherst agrees. She is dismayed when plants are released under a certain hardiness zone and end up being relabeled for a much warmer zone. She had this experience with *Coreopsis* 'Limerock Ruby': "I felt

Massachusetts Horticultural Society

Every self-respecting gardener in the Northeast knows of the Massachusetts Horticultural Society (MHS), founded in 1829. One of the services the MHS offers is a HortLine staffed by knowledgeable MHS master gardeners who can answer a lot of your questions. You can reach them at (617) 933–4929 Monday, Wednesday, and Friday 10:00 A.M. to 2:00 P.M., and on Saturday 10:00 A.M to 2:00 P.M. from May to September only. And believe me, if they don't know the answer to your question, they will find it. Visit "MassHort," as some call it, online at www.masshort.org.

bad for all the customers who bought it, thinking it would be a perennial for them." Now we know to treat it as an annual.

Barbara Provest, a Massachusetts Horticultural Society (MHS) master gardener in Framingham, puts it succinctly: "I would like a nickel for every plant sold to me as 'hardy' that never made it through the first winter or two."

Planting for your conditions is the best advice I can give. The saying "right plant in the right place" is particularly apt when gardening with perennials. Check in with your gardening neighbors, local nursery, or nearby botanical garden. If your neighbor has luck with a certain plant, chances are you will, too.

Designing with Perennials

Most perennials do not bloom all summer. This makes designing with perennials an exciting challenge. I don't particularly mind if my plants are not in bloom all the time because I have a real soft spot for foliage color and texture. But if you want constant flower color in your garden, design your garden for a constant succession of bloom. Learn the bloom time of each perennial and choose plants that flower at different times in the spring, summer, and fall. By artfully staggering the plants' locations through the border, you lead the eye from bloom to bloom all season long.

Barbara's Border for Constant Color

I designed these herbaceous perennials into a Zone 6a border for a succession of bloom. They all require sun to light shade.

Plant	Bloom Time	Color
Daffodil (*Narcissus*)	April–May	Yellow
Candytuft (*Iberis sempervirens*)	April–June	White
Bleeding heart (*Dicentra spectabilis*)	April–June	Deep pink
Lady's mantle (*Alchemilla mollis*)	May–June	Chartreuse and green
Ornamental onion (*Allium aflatunense*)	May–June	Purple
Cornflower (*Centaurea*)	May–July	Blue
Catnip (*Nepeta mussini*)	May–October	Lavender and gray
Meadow sage (*Salvia* x *superba*)	May–October	Blue
Queen-of-the-prairie (*Filipendula rubra*)	July–September	Lavender
Snakeroot (*Eupatorium rugosum*)	August–October	White

You can have fun by planning gardens with different color themes in different months. You can choose colors that would look horrible if they bloomed together, but because they don't bloom at the same time they don't clash. Or you may want the look of a monochromatic garden, like the all-white garden at Sissinghurst in England. You can design with just one plant like daylilies, irises, or hostas—all of which have varieties with slightly different bloom times. You can design a mixed border that is predominantly perennials but that is offset by the structure of shrubs and filled in with constantly blooming annuals. Shrubs like hydrangea, butterfly bush (*Buddleia*), and deutszia work well in these designs.

You may want a garden that peaks in spring or a garden designed specifically for the fall. Your choices may depend on where you spend your time at different times of the year. My spring garden is in the front of my house, where I can see it from the living room, which is where we've spent a good deal of the winter in front of the fire. The summer and fall gardens and the cutting garden are at the back of the house so we can view them from the kitchen and deck, where we spend the summers.

Sun or Shade?

Some books say that the best site for a perennial border is in full sun—that is, six to eight hours of sun per day. I think that limits your choices: There are so many perennials that like the shade or partial shade. Just take a walk around the shady gardens of the New England Wild Flower Society's Garden in the Woods in Framingham (see chapter 12) or the shady areas in the ten acres at Allen C. Haskell Horticulturists in New Bedford. Or read books on shade-loving perennials, like Ken Druse's *The Natural Shade Garden*. You'll see what I mean.

Here are some choice and lesser-known shade lovers, recommended by Leo Blanchette of the Zone 6a Blanchette Gardens in Carlisle.

Mukdenia rossii. This attractive plant has white flowers in May. The broad leaves are a deep green until late August. When cool weather approaches the foliage turns burgundy. It likes a rich, well-drained soil in the shade, preferring moisture but tolerating drier locations. It grows to 12 inches high.

Peonies (*Paeonia japonica* and *P. obovata*). Most peonies appreciate a spot in the sun, where they can remain undisturbed for years, but *P. japonica* grows best in light shade. It has a white flower. *P. obovata* is pink with a single flower and may need shade, Blanchette says.

Solomon's seal (*Polygonatum odoratum* 'Grace Barker' and 'Red Legs'). These May bloomers like a shady, well-drained, humus-rich site. "*P. odoratum* 'Grace Barker' has leaves that are streaked white. *P. odoratum* 'Red Legs' is our introduction. It has red stems."

Pheasant's eye (*Adonis amurensis*). This plant blooms in March. "Plant it behind taller, later-blooming perennials because the light green foliage disappears as summer approaches and the plant goes dormant," Blanchette says. "They grow best in a light shade garden with well-drained soil."

Syneilesis aconitifolia **and** *S. palmate*. These Asian natives offer attractive, deeply cut, umbrella-like foliage. They need rich, well-drained soil.

Mayapple (*Podophyllum hexandrum*). The Asian species has single pale pink flowers and large leaves. It grows to 18 inches in clumps, preferring a rich, woodland soil.

Twinleaf (*Jeffersonia dubia*). "The flowers only last a few days, but the wonderful foliage persists the full season," Blanchette says. "Grown in a well-drained, rich soil, it still takes a while to get fully established. This one has blue flowers in spring."

Borders or Islands?

Most gardening books, English or American, show perennial borders against some sort of backdrop—a hedge, fence, or shrubs—because that was how borders were traditionally placed until Alan Bloom of Bressingham's in England decided to bring a perennial border out into the middle of the garden as an "island bed."

Whether a single border set against a backdrop, or a double border with a walkway between, traditional beds are usually designed to be seen from only one side—the front. The island bed is meant to be seen from every angle, which is trickier to design. Traditional one-sided borders usually have taller plants at the back, gradating down in size to the low, mounding plants at the front. The edges can be crisp, straight, and formal or soft and undulating with plants like catnip (*Nepeta*) and lady's mantle (*Alchemilla mollis*) or low-growing candytuft (*Iberis*) flopping over the edge for a softer effect. Sometimes a garden object such as a tepee with climbing plants can establish the focal point for height, particularly in an island bed.

Whether you choose a border or an island bed, cluster your plants in groups of three or five and carry the groups through the border so your bed is more than a collection of "one of everything." Groupings draw the eye along the border. Plant form, structure, and foliage are just as important as flower color. Each plant should be interesting to look at after its blooms have passed. When using plants like ornamental onion (*Allium*), where the foliage dies back even while the plant is in bloom, then be sure that another plant (like hosta) comes fast behind to mask the spent foliage. Consider using a tall, transparent plant, such as *Verbena bonariensis*, occasionally in the front. Transparent plants create a veil through which one sees the rest of the border—they give height and color without blocking the view.

Designing with perennials is often about mixing in other plants. Michel Marcellot of Seven Arrows Farm in Attleboro explains that the older he gets, the more value he sees in evergreens, both for their utility in keeping the garden vibrant look-ing in winter and for their use as a visual anchor or base for the design of a garden. "I highly recommend starting with an ever-green base for any new design," he says. "As much as 80 percent of the garden should be evergreen, with deciduous and herba-ceous plants making up the difference. The calming effect of sub-tle differences in form, foliage color, and texture is vastly underrated."

Containers

Perennials can be grown in containers for the deck or front porch, but most places in Massachusetts you would need to bring the containers into the house or a greenhouse to overwinter the plants, if you have room. Container perennials should have strong foliage or structural interest because the blooms won't last. Bergenia, for example, looks super in a container—its architec-tural leaves and red stems look good even when its pink flowers have gone by.

Acquiring Perennials

Note that I write "acquiring" and not "buying." Perennials often grow to such a size that they need to be divided, and that's when gardeners start looking to give away divisions. Pass-along plants are great if the plant is something you want. But "buyer beware": This generosity may not always work in your favor. Maybe the plant is too vigorous, and in two years' time you'll have to divide and dispose of it. A plant like gooseneck loosestrife (*Lysimachia*), once in your garden, may never leave! Make sure you know the characteristics of what you're being offered. And acquaint your-self with the state list of invasive plants (see chapter 9). You don't want to introduce these offenders to your garden.

Other ways to acquire perennials are by propagating them (easiest from cuttings), growing them from seed, and purchasing.

Buy from a reputable nursery, know what you're looking for by the foliage, and trust the label. (Chances are the perennial will not be in bloom when you locate it.) Look closely at the foliage to ensure the plant is healthy. Yellowed, shriveled, spotted, or insect-damaged leaves are signs of problems. Leave those plants behind. Tap a plant out of its pot to make sure the roots are healthy.

Perennial Care

The roots of perennials often grow deep. In the case of peonies, for instance, the roots extend down as much as 2 feet. You can constantly improve and amend the soil in an annual or vegetable bed, but it's hard to make changes or improvements to an established perennial bed without disturbing what's already growing there.

For that reason, prepare the perennial bed deeply and thoroughly at the outset. Adjust the soil pH and add organic amendments as necessary to improve the soil tilth, texture, and condition (refer to chapter 1). Perennials won't like being constantly disturbed once they are established. Fall is a good time to prepare a new perennial bed. This gives the organic material and microbes time to settle in and do their work before you plant in the spring.

Pay attention to the size the plant will become. It's tempting to build a new perennial bed by thickly planting perennials so that the bed looks finished. I know because I've done it. New plants look small. It's hard to believe that something in a gallon container will grow to be the size of a small shrub in two years. Resist the temptation to plant too closely—fill in with annuals if you don't like the sparse look of a newly installed border.

Before putting plants into the ground, water each perennial well in its pot, ideally the day before planting. Dig a hole that accommodates the full spread of the plant's roots: "a hundred-dollar hole for a ten-dollar plant." Sprinkle in a little slow-release organic fertilizer to give the plant a nutrient boost. Plant the

crown of the plant at soil level—which may not be the way the plant currently sits in the nursery pot. Then water the plant in. Keep the soil moist for the first week or two, after which you can ease off and establish a regular watering routine (see chapter 3). You may want to cut or pinch back a plant with heavy top growth so that its energy goes into the roots rather than the foliage. Perennials don't always look fabulous when they're first planted. They look better the second year and come into their own from year three onward.

Transplanting

In general, the best time to transplant a perennial, whether spring blooming or fall blooming, is after it has finished blooming. But some late fall-blooming perennials, like boltonia, may prefer to be transplanted in the spring. Shallow-rooted perennials, like heuchera or astilbe, may also prefer to be transplanted in the spring because they are prone to heaving out of the soil if planted too late in the year. They need time to establish a good base before the cold of winter hits. You can transplant in the middle of summer, but you will have to pamper the plant with extra care and water. It will have a tougher time establishing itself unless well cared for. Certain plants (like irises) go dormant after they have bloomed and can be divided at that time—usually late spring or early summer.

I tend to think that if the plant is unaware that it's being moved, it will settle in quickly no matter when I move it. I dig up more soil around the plant than is really necessary so that I disturb its roots as little as possible, and I always have the receiving bed prepared. When I slide the plant into the new hole, I don't think the plant is even aware that it's been moved.

Keep records of what you planted when and where. I can't tell you the number of times I've dug up my lovely white 'Thalia' daffodils in the fall because I've gone to plant something right where the daffodils are slumbering.

Perennials for All Places

No matter what your hardiness zone, there are remarkable perennials just right for your Massachusetts garden. Here are recommendations from the experts.

Zone 5

Jacqueline Cowles of Andrew's Greenhouse in Amherst offers this list of her personal favorites:

Barrenwort (*Epimedium rubrum*).

Catnip (*Nepeta yunnanensis*). "Hummingbirds find this plant irresistible."

Willow blue star (*Amsonia tabernamontana*). Pale blue flowers sit atop arching clumps of glossy, willowlike leaves. "It finishes blooming by the end of June," Cowles says, "but the foliage stays in great condition all through summer and turns a golden hue in fall."

Indian physic (*Gillenia trifoliata*). "This North American native produces a profusion of small star-shaped white flowers held on erect, slender stems. It is a most elegant and graceful plant."

Glaucidium palmatum. "A choice Japanese woodlander with maplelike, large-lobed leaves and silky, purple pink flowers reminiscent of a single peony," she explains.

Greater burnet (*Pimpinella major* 'Rosea'). "It looks very much like a pink Queen Anne's lace. It is sophisticated, unobtrusive, and gentle in nature."

Coneflower (*Echinacea* 'White Swan'). "This workhorse is never out of flowers until some hard frosts," Cowles reports.

Lady fern (*Athyrium filix-femina* x *niponicum* 'Branford Rambler'). "A polite spreader with the beautiful varigation of the painted fern and the strength of the lady fern."

Thyme (*Thymus pulegoides* 'Dot Well's Creeping'). "A great culinary and ornamental thyme variety with rich green foliage and lavender flowers."

Cranesbill (*Geranium* 'Philipe Vapelle'). This hardy, dependable performer doesn't need to be cut back after blooming.

Bleeding heart (*Dicentra spectabilis* 'Gold Heart'). With its golden foliage, "this one is unique."

Zone 6a

In Hopkinton, Ruth Langh of Ruth Langh Garden Design highlights her favorite plants:

- Variegated Solomon's seal (*Polygonatum odoratum* 'Variegatum')

- Cranesbill (*Geranium macrorrhizum* 'Spessart')

- Blue false indigo (*Baptisia australis*)

- *Iris cristata*

- Catnip (*Nepeta siberica* 'Souvenir D'Andre Chaudron')

- Black cohosh (*Cimicifuga racemosa*)

- Fringed bleeding heart (*Dicentra eximia*)

- Hostas

Plants that have not done well for Langh (even though all the literature said they would) include certain azaleas that were not bud hardy and never bloomed (probably grown farther south and then imported to Massachusetts); most astilbes ("they crinkle up in the least bit of dryness"); creeping euonymus, which gets crown gall disease too frequently; and lily-of-the-valley bush (*Pieris japonica*), which gets covered with lace bug when grown in full sun.

Zone 6b

"We have grown so many perennials over the years, many of which have lasted only a year or two and then slowly dissolved or disappeared," says Kathy Tracey of Avant Gardens in North Dartmouth. In her opinion, these are the best perennials for southern New England and, she says, the list "only includes plants that have greeted us with vigor each subsequent spring and that have either an extended period of bloom or great foliage, or both."

Calamint (*Calamintha nepetoides*). "Slow-growing, with pink flowers and lovely fragrance," Tracey says.

Cranesbill: *Geranium* x 'Jolly Bee', with masses of long-blooming blue flowers, and *G.* x *cantabrigiense* 'St. Ola', a white-flowered evergreen geranium that makes a nice ground cover.

Hyssop (*Agastache* 'Blue Fortune'). "Long bloom of soft pale blue spikes—heat and drought tolerant."

Fleeceflower: *Persicaria amplexicaulis* 'Golden Arrow', for late summer/fall bloom of narrow crimson tassels on great foliage, and *P. polymorpha,* for size and long bloomtime of fleecy white flowers.

False indigo (*Baptisia*). The new cultivars are long lived, reminiscent of lupines in appearance, Tracey says.

Upright wild ginger (*Saruma henryi*). "Fuzzy light green leaves with yellow flowers. Underutilized for shade," she says.

Siberian bugloss (*Brunnera macrophylla* 'Jack Frost'). "Exceptional foliage of silver leaves with bright blue flowers."

Sedge (*Carex* 'Ice Dance'). With its dark green blades edged in white, this sedge is a great ground cover for shade or partial sun.

Yellow wax bells (*Kirengeshoma palmate*). An erect, clump-forming plant with reddish purple stems and pale green leaves.

Cohosh (*Cimicifuga* 'Hillside Black Beauty', Black Negligee', or 'James Compton'). Handsome, dark-leaved selections.

At Seven Arrows Farm in Attleboro, Judy Marcellot recommends her selection of choice perennials for Zone 6b:

Sweet coltsfoot *(Petasites gigantea)*. "Best planted in a shaded moist, boggy spot," she says. "Afternoon sun will wilt the plants, so plan to avoid strong afternoon sun."

Toad lilies *(Tricyrtis)*. "These mostly arching, pendulous toad lilies are a great source of fall color," Marcellot states. "Beautiful, subtle and sophisticated, they come in flower colors from bright white, striking violet, to deep dark purple. They make mums look like plastic party favors."

Joe-pye weed (*Eupatorium maculatum* 'Gateway'). "A tall drink of water! This 6-foot fountain of pink in the June/July garden is something not to miss." For best impact, "combine it with dark-foliage, medium-height plants at its base, like *Ligularia* 'Brit Marie Crawford', dark-foliage heuchera, or *Euphorbia* 'Chameleon' or 'Fireglow'."

Lobelia 'Grape Knee Hi' and *L.* 'Monet Moment'. "Bomb-proof" late-season color and vigor.

Arisemea **and other aroids.** "The dragon-headed flowers of the cobra lily comes in sizes ranging from the diminutive mouse plant (*Arisarum proboscideum*) to the giant *Arisaema heterophyllum*. These are great shade plants for naturalizing, creating an Zen-like feel to a shady spot or a woodland garden," Marcellot states.

Perennial Maintenance

Weeds compete for everything—nutrients, water, air, space. Get rid of them! Simple as that. We used to be taught to cultivate the

soil vigorously—always. But vigorous cultivation may destroy soil texture, bring weed seeds to the surface, or snap off weeds so that their roots remain in the soil and multiply. I'm still dealing with chickweed that in my younger gardening days I did not remove correctly (see chapter 10 for details of proper weed treatment). The best approach is to loosen the soil simply by inserting a fork in the soil between plants and gently moving the fork back and forth. This motion opens up the soil and makes it easier to uproot weeds, and it doesn't overly disturb what's growing.

Depending on weather, your perennials may need regular watering. Then there's the deadheading, pinching, debudding, pruning, staking, and cutting back. These all make the plant look nicer and help it put energy into root growth and new bushy upper growth.

Should you cut back top growth in autumn? A late-fall cleanup of herbaceous perennials has benefits—it tidies the garden and cuts down on chores in the spring. But leaving some stems up through winter gives the garden visual definition and provides food and protection for wildlife. I like to see the seed-heads of coneflower (*Echinacea*), Jerusalem artichoke (*Helianthus tuberosus*), and black-eyed Susan (*Rudbeckia*). I'm prepared for the extra work in the spring—it's a tradeoff.

Woody perennials like Russian sage (*Perovskia*), catmint (*Nepeta*), or lavender (*Lavandula*) do not respond well to being cut back in the fall. They may even die. Woody perennials are best pruned of deadwood in spring once you see a substantial flush of new growth.

Part of garden maintenance is keeping an eye out for problems caused by pests and diseases. You can minimize problems by keeping plants healthy, planting them in the right conditions, and treating them well.

There is nothing more exciting than seeing a perennial bed come alive each spring. The ground almost pulsates with energy. There are bittersweet moments. Perhaps your favorite Russian sage didn't make it through the winter. But then you look to your right and see last year's new cranesbill (*Geranium*) starting to show through—and you smile. Perennials just keep on giving.

Vegetable Gardening

Before you even put vegetable seed into soil, think about your gardening goals and then plan. Don't wing it with vegetables—you'll waste time and resources and may end up with a scrappy crop. What are the steps to growing good vegetables in Massachusetts? Decide where to locate the garden—its proper site. Assess what size garden you want to work and in what design. Choose what vegetables to grow—a combination of what you like and what grows well in Massachusetts. Cultivate your crop.

The good news is even if you're short on time or space, you can still grow vegetables. You can design them into your flower and shrub borders or grow them in containers. You can have any size vegetable garden, from huge to teeny. An older gentleman who lives near me has a tiny vegetable garden—two 10-by-4-foot beds raised 4 feet high to make tending them easier on his back, and all enclosed with a little picket fence. It's exactly what he needs, and it is a showpiece.

Most vegetables need six to eight hours of sunlight a day and prefer eight to ten hours. Fruiting vegetables like tomatoes, peppers, or squash need a full day of sun. Root vegetables like carrots or beets can tolerate less, and leafy vegetables like lettuce can handle quite a lot of shade.

South-facing beds are optimum. A slight slope is good. If you have steep slopes, consider terracing. Don't locate the garden at the bottom of a hill where cold air and water collect.

For ease of harvesting, situate a vegetable garden near the kitchen. Locate the garden near a source of water, such as a spigot, or bring a hose outlet extension to the garden. Install rain barrels to collect extra rainfall (see chapter 3).

If your site is windy, protect your crops. The wind can dry out or batter them. Build protection in the form of built structures or shrubs, keeping these protective elements at a height that won't reduce available sunlight, and make them permeable to let air through.

The best soil for vegetables is deep, moist, and friable, with abundant organic material and microbial life. Different crops like a slightly different pH, and you may need to adjust soil accordingly (see chapter 2). Well-draining soil is important. Vegetables don't like wet feet and tend to develop root rot and fungal diseases if kept too damp. If you have poorly draining soil, consider building raised beds for better drainage.

Garden Design

The size of your vegetable garden will be dictated by a number of factors, the first being the size of the site. If you have only 3 square feet of yard in full sun, that's the size of your garden—unless you're able to remove nearby trees or fences to open up a larger area. Consider your work and family schedule; how much time you have to devote to the garden? And finally, evaluate what you plan to grow in the garden. If you want only lettuce, tomatoes, and a few herbs, then you won't need a huge bed—you could get by with containers. But if you plan to incorporate four compost areas, a greenhouse, corn, asparagus, squash, and an assortment of climbing vegetables, then you will need a lot of space.

You can design your vegetable garden in any configuration: straight rows, square beds, circles—or a combination of these. The primary concern is to give your plants the right amount of space to thrive. Research each vegetable variety's recommended spacing, measured from the center of one plant to the center of another. You want the garden to be efficient. You want to be able to reach your vegetables without clambering around the garden, compacting the soil and damaging your soaker hoses. And you want chores like weeding to be as easy as possible. But have fun—it's *your* garden.

Contained raised beds can be built to a variety of levels—even waist high. Soil drains well in raised beds, warms up more quickly in spring, and retains warmth longer in fall. It's easy to reach weeds and harvest vegetables. Raised beds also look neat, clean, and efficient.

Uncontained mounded rows are easy to create. You can use the "lasagna" method: Spread a thick layer of newspapers on the ground, top with a layer of humus-rich soil, and then plant. Mounded rows offer similar benefits to raised beds, though they don't look quite as neat. Water drains well from the beds but may collect in the pathways, and runoff may lead to soil erosion.

Sunken trenches hold water and therefore may not drain well. They are also are hard work to create.

Out-of-the-box designs like circles, triangles, or ovals can have the positives of all the other designs if designed well. You can also make these raised beds. And they are fun.

I like to experiment, so I have tried most of these designs. I do like waist-high raised beds because they are easy on the back.

What to Grow

Grow what you want to eat and only enough for your family and friends. It sounds obvious, but it's easy to get carried away when the catalogs arrive in winter. Before you know it, you've ordered all sorts of vegetables that your family won't touch.

Probably the most important things to consider when growing vegetables in Massachusetts are temperature ranges and frost dates, which dictate the length of the growing season. This season can be fairly short in the cooler northern corner of the state. Warm-season vegetables may be available for only a short period of time up there.

Beets, cabbage, carrots, garlic, kale, lettuce, onions, potatoes, snap peas, and Swiss chard grow well anywhere in Massachusetts, states Julie Rawson of Many Hands Organic Farm in Barre. Less common—but still easy to grow—vegetables for Massachusetts include Asian greens of all sorts, celery, cilantro, collards, leeks, and parsley, she says.

Climate will influence your choices. Rawson can grow greens through the summer in central Massachusetts, where they get abundant rainfall. "We can't grow cranberries, which have a specific need for the climate of southeast Massachusetts." In warmer parts of the state, "you can grow heat-tolerant varieties of the cool-temperature crops like lettuce and broccoli," says Frank Albani Jr. of Plymouth.

Steve Bellavia and Tony Vinci of Johnny's Selected Seeds in Maine recommend some lesser-known veggies. "There are so many vegetables that folks don't think to grow because they are less common, but they grow well in Massachusetts," says Bellavia.

Chicory. "It should be more widely used," Vinci says.

Fava beans. "These are so tasty and very popular in Middle Eastern food," says Bellavia. They are best when young. When old they get a bit tough.

Renee Shepherd of Renee's Garden is an expert purveyor of superior garden seeds. She recommends the following vegetable cultivars that have been particular favorites of her Massachusetts customers:

- Spinach: 'Baby Leaf Catalina'
- Bush bean: 'Slenderette' and 'Tricolor'
- Lettuce: 'Monet's Garden' mesclun
- Cucumbers: 'Chelsea Prize'
- Cherry tomatoes: 'Garden Candy' and 'Camp Joy'
- Beets: 'Jewel-Toned'
- Swiss chard: 'Bright Lights'
- Kale: 'Lacinato'
- Snap peas: 'Super Sugar'
- Zucchini: 'Tricolor'
- Chile peppers: red and orange habanero

Gai lan. "If more people tried this, they would grow less broccoli," Vinci states.

Jerusalem artichoke. Harvest this after frost, Vinci recommends.

Kale. "It's not just for garnishes around salad bars," Vinci says. It's a tasty green on its own.

Okra. This can be grown in New England if you choose an early variety. Bellavia suggests 'Cajun Delight'. Vinci calls okra a "wonderful, misunderstood veggie."

Scorzonera and salsify. Interest in root vegetables is growing, Bellavia notes. "These are both nice."

Shell beans. This old-time favorite is not commonly grown these days. "They are easy to grow and delicious, and it's hard to find them at the market," Bellavia says.

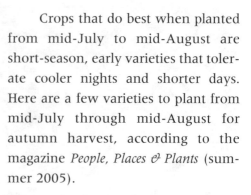

Crops that do best when planted from mid-July to mid-August are short-season, early varieties that tolerate cooler nights and shorter days. Here are a few varieties to plant from mid-July through mid-August for autumn harvest, according to the magazine *People, Places & Plants* (summer 2005).

- Beets: 'Early Wonder'
- Carrots: 'Nelson'
- Kale: 'Red Russian'
- Lettuce: 'Winter Density'
- Swiss chard: 'Bright Lights'

Planting

Some vegetable seeds can be sown directly in the ground as soon as the ground can be worked, such as peas, beets, lettuce, onions, and radishes. Others are seeded directly in the ground only after the danger of frost has passed. If your growing season is shorter, as in the western part of the state, you may need to start plants such as tomatoes, brussels sprouts, or cauliflower indoors and set them out when there is no danger of frost.

Seed packets have most of the information you need to know on the back: when to plant, how to care for the plant, and when to harvest it. Each plant has an optimum soil temperature for germination and an optimum soil temperature for growing. A soil thermometer is a handy tool. If the temperature is not right, the seed will either not germinate or the plant will take so long getting established that it becomes weak. And the temperature at which a plant germinates may not be the temperature a plant needs to grow and thrive. The wrong temperature will slow growth or result in a spindly, weak plant susceptible to disease. For instance, tomatoes germinate best at around 60 degrees but grow better at 80 degrees. Lettuce likes cool temperatures; it won't germinate well when the soil temperatures gets above 65 degrees, and it won't germinate above 75 degrees. Pepper and eggplant seeds prefer 85 degrees but the plants grow well at 75 degrees. Harden off your plants before you put them in the ground. See chapter 4 for more seed-starting and cultivation tips.

Seed Sources

These sources of tried-and-true vegetables for Massachusetts gardens come from Julie Rawson of Many Hands Organic Farm in Barre.

- Johnny's Selected Seeds: www.johnnyseeds.com
- Fedco Co-op Seeds: www.fedcoseeds.com
- Renee Shepherd's Seeds: www.reneesgarden.com
- High Mowing Organic Seeds: www.highmowingseeds.com
- The Cook's Garden: www.cooksgarden.com

There are different techniques to planting vegetables: crop rotation, succession planting, interplanting, and companion planting. Each method has sound reasoning behind it. You can choose one approach or combine them.

Crop Rotation

The idea behind crop rotation is that vegetables from the same botanical family should not be grown in the same spot every year. Why? Each vegetable family is susceptible to certain pests and diseases. Insect larvae and diseases often remain in the soil after a crop has been harvested, waiting to attack the same crop the next year. If you plant something from a different family in that soil each year for the next three or so years, you can outwit the enemy. By the time crop number one comes around again, with luck all of that family's enemies will be gone from that patch of soil or at least substantially decreased.

Additionally, different crops use up different nutrients in the soil. If you plant the same crop in the same soil year after year, eventually you will find them getting weaker and weaker because they are deprived of the nutrients they need. You could amend the soil for specific nutrients, but it's easier to rotate. Some crops, like legumes, actually improve the soil; rotating them through the garden will improve the soil in each bed they are planted.

Here's a sample crop rotation: Say we rotate through four beds (A, B, C, and D). You plant members of the same vegetable family in plot A the first year, then move the entire family of vegetables (whatever you want to plant from that family) to plot B in the second year, then plot C the third year, and plot D the fourth

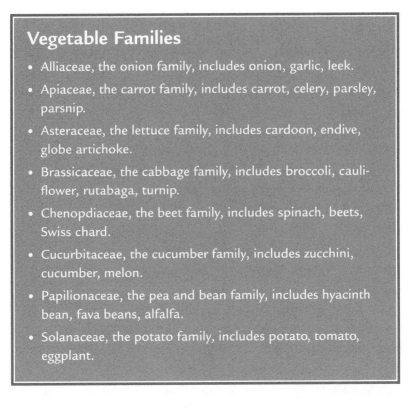

Vegetable Families

- Alliaceae, the onion family, includes onion, garlic, leek.
- Apiaceae, the carrot family, includes carrot, celery, parsley, parsnip.
- Asteraceae, the lettuce family, includes cardoon, endive, globe artichoke.
- Brassicaceae, the cabbage family, includes broccoli, cauliflower, rutabaga, turnip.
- Chenopdiaceae, the beet family, includes spinach, beets, Swiss chard.
- Cucurbitaceae, the cucumber family, includes zucchini, cucumber, melon.
- Papilionaceae, the pea and bean family, includes hyacinth bean, fava beans, alfalfa.
- Solanaceae, the potato family, includes potato, tomato, eggplant.

year, so that they don't arrive back in plot A until year five.

Factor in the height and size of what you're planting so that the crop fits into the rotation but doesn't crowd or block the sun from others nearby. Some vegetables with large foliage (like pumpkins) help suppress weeds. Switching them in rotation will help keep the weed population down. But their large foliage can also create too much shade for smaller plants.

In a crop rotation schedule, you also have to factor in the different pH needs plants have. But plants with different nutritional needs can be planted together—light feeders like carrots work well with heavy feeders like tomatoes.

You will need to keep good notes to remember what you had where from year to year. Planning a rotation schedule, drawing it out ahead of time, and keeping excellent notes will save headaches and frustration in the future.

Succession Planting

Succession planting is simply scheduling one crop to follow another. If you want to have vegetables all season long, you plant an early crop, then a mid-season crop, and then a fall crop so that the garden is in use at all times. It can be of the same vegetable: spring carrots and then summer carrots, which mature in the fall. Or you can plant different vegetables to mature at different times throughout the growing season. The longer your growing season, the more time you have to plant several crops of the same vegetable. An early crop of bush beans, for example, can be harvested and a second crop planted for harvesting later in the season. Don't plant from the same family in the same place more than twice in a season for the reasons given earlier in crop rotation—possible pest and disease contamination of the soil.

The idea is that gardeners don't need to stop planting just because spring has passed. Late-summer planting fills in the holes and takes us through to fall. Just make sure you plant in time for the crop to reach maturity before the first killing frost.

Cool-weather crops are those that do not tolerate heat. They are planted as early-spring crops. Crops such as broccoli, brussels sprouts, garlic, peas, and onions can be planted twenty to forty days before the last frost. Beets, carrots, cauliflower, lettuce can be planted ten to thirty days before the last frost. Cool-season plants that mature quickly can be sown again in late summer for fall harvest, such as lettuce, peas, and turnips.

Warm-weather crops need warmer temperatures. Sweet potatoes, eggplant, and tomatoes are planted later in the spring, after the soil has warmed to a minimum of 60 to 65 degrees. Snap beans, lima beans, sweet corn, and cucumber should be planted on or after the last frost date.

Julie Rawson's gardens in Barre are at 1,000 feet elevation. The nights are often down in the 40s through June and then again by the third week in August. Rawson starts the planting season with peas and onions and spinach around April 15. "The trick is to succession plant throughout the season," she says. "I don't put out tender things until the first week in June, and some crops like peppers and eggplants around June 15. I plant out my last greens and lettuce around the first week of September." Garlic is her final planting, on November 1.

Interplanting

Interplanting is simply growing two or more crops in the same place. The Native Americans interplanted with corn, pole beans, and squash—the corn became the pole for the beans and a protective windbreak for the low-growing squash. Interplanting makes the most efficient use of space and can cut down on chores which, of course, saves time.

Sow crops that grow at different rates. Plant a slow-growing crop, one that has the potential to take up a lot of space when mature, together with a faster-growing crop that will be mature and harvested by the time the first one reaches maturity. Early beets and winter squash are good examples. Interplanting is also useful when one plant that doesn't like the heat, like lettuce, can be shaded and cooled by the other plant. Swiss chard, for instance, planted close to tomatoes, shades the soil and helps to moderate the temperature. Deep-rooted parsnips work well when planted with shallow-rooted onions.

Companion Planting

Plants are said to have adversaries and friends that help or harm each other. By clever planting you offer each plant the protection of the other. For instance, the friends to brussels sprouts are beets, bush beans, lettuce, and nasturtium; its adversaries are kohlrabi and strawberry. Friends to carrot are beans, chives, leeks, onions, and tomatoes; its adversaries are celery and parsnip. Louise Riotte has written in detail about companion planting in her two books, *Carrots Love Tomatoes* and *Roses Love Garlic*. Rodale's *Companion Planting* is also an excellent read if you're interested in the subject.

Tending Your Crops

Tending a vegetable garden is a most satisfying endeavor. At the end of the day you have delicious, homegrown food.

Watering. Vegetables need regular watering, but the critical times for watering are when the plants are seedlings, when they are about to set flowers, and when they are about to set fruit. Water is essential for leaf and shoot growth, but too much water can slow production of fruit and diminish flavor. Refer to chapter 3 for more details about watering.

Feeding. Test your vegetable garden soil every few years to be sure enough nutrients are available. Certain crops are heavy feeders: Asparagus, cabbage, corn, and eggplant can use an extra boost through the season. Wood ash or bonemeal helps root vegetables. A fertilizer like fish emulsion will incorporate more nitrogen in the soil to benefit leafy crops like lettuce. These fish and seaweed fertilizers are well-balanced natural fertilizers and provide the major nutrients (N-P-K) and a lot of the minor elements, too. Don't use animal manure on vegetable gardens because of the potential for the transmission of disease pathogens.

Weeding. Weeds compete with vegetables for water, nutrients, air, and space. Take the time to weed, even if you put in only an hour a day. Don't wait until weeds have gone to seed, or you will be weeding forever.

Keeping plants healthy. Make the garden unappealing to pests and diseases by cleaning up debris and cutting back dead foliage. If your plant is damaged or sick, research what is wrong promptly—before the problem spreads (see chapter 10). I believe that people should not spray vegetables with chemical fertilizers, insecticides, or herbicides. You are going to put these plants into your body.

Good soil, sound watering practices, and impeccable hygiene are the best defenses against pests and disease. The end result is a satisfying bowl of homegrown vegetables on the dinner table for your friends and family.

Trees and Shrubs

Trees and shrubs are long-term investments. You want to choose the right varieties for your Massachusetts garden. Most trees and shrubs recommended for Zones 5 to 7 will do well someplace in the state, but do your research. That favorite species you've seen growing in the northern Berkshires may—or may not—do equally well at your home on Martha's Vineyard.

What is the difference between a tree and a shrub? For starters, the number of stems, or trunks. Trees have one stem, and shrubs usually have two or more. And size somewhat determines what category a woody plant falls in. The silverbell tree (*Halesia*), for instance, could be treated either like a large shrub or small tree. Some dogwoods (*Cornus* spp.) are multistemmed and look like big shrubs; and franklinia and stewartia are in between. Throughout this chapter I will refer mostly to trees, but you can assume I also mean shrubs unless I state otherwise.

Woody plants, or "woodies," as they are affectionately called, serve many purposes in the landscape.

- For visual aesthetic appeal.
- For the simple pleasure of relaxing under the spreading branches.
- To add structure and form.
- To create a barrier or hedge for privacy; to keep people out or animals in.

• For utilitarian purposes: to serve as a windbreak, provide shade, or hide an eyesore like an air-conditioning unit.

Soil, drainage, sun exposure, climate, and wind affect the survival of trees and shrubs. Select a tree that is adapted to your site conditions and hardiness zone. Consider the cultivar's mature size. Trees and shrubs can get huge! Give a sapling the space it will need at maturity—even if you don't expect to be around then.

Buying a tree is an investment in time and money. It's expensive to remove a mistake. I recommend that you visit one or two arboretums to see trees in their mature state, to see what their foliage is like in the different seasons, or to learn about their shape in the winter. Visit nurseries that carry mature stock. Look around the historic district of your town. No matter how gorgeous photos are in books, they don't give an adequate picture of a tree or shrub and its shape in relation to other plants. Do your research. It's not a bad idea to seek the advice of a professional landscape architect, landscape designer, or arborist. You can hire a professional for an hour or two to walk around your property and recommend varieties that suit your property and personality or to visit a nursery with you. You can also ask for referrals from your local garden center, request the names of arborists who work at nearby arboretums, or call your town hall to speak to the tree warden in your community. (Chapter 12, resources, lists sources of professional help.)

Great Trees for a Great State

Landscape designer and lifelong naturalist Jim Kiely of Medford believes that all properties should be designed as complex, organic systems. "It is time to get over the fear of planting large trees," he says, "particularly those that once dotted the wild New England landscape." He recommends these great varieties:

American elm (*Ulmus americana* 'Princeton' and 'Valley Forge'). "News flash! You can grow elm trees!" Kiely asserts. These two varieties are resistant to Dutch elm disease. "Fast growing, vase shaped, cathedral in size, salt tolerant, and unmoved by the wind, they will keep your house coolly shaded during the summer, turn modest yellow in autumn, and live peaceably with a wide range of understory plants. At a mature size of about 70 by 50 feet, one tree is all you'll need to benefit from its effects and to help revitalize this great American icon."

Red or Norway pine (*Pinus resinosa*). "The people of Minnesota had the good sense to adopt this as their state tree, which proves that government can make good decisions," Kiely quips. This two-needled pine "thrives in sunny, dry soil, provides high shade, and has a pastel red plated bark that warms the soul in winter and cools it in the dog days of August. Use this straight, 65-by-25-foot wonder as a windbreak and to make your neighbors jealous. It is salt intolerant and looks best in groups or with other evergreens."

Bald cypress (*Taxodium distichum*). "Move over swamp maples. For certainly within New England's wetlands and moisture-retaining soils there is a place for this deciduous conifer," he says. This native tree offers fibrous reddish brown bark and feathery needles that turn bright yellow in autumn. "It reaches a size of about 60 by 25 feet, and its female, 1-inch cones appear like sleigh bells at the tips of its branches."

River birch (*Betula nigra*). "Perhaps the best shade tree of all the birches, this native's peeling gray-, salmon-, and lavender-tinged bark is certainly among the loveliest for a designed land-scape," Kiely says. It grows to 60 by 40 feet, with single- and multiple-trunk forms. Plant it in spring in a nonalkaline, sunny location, and give it ample water at first. "Birches need cool root zones, so mulching this specimen and combining it with low-growing shrubs are necessities. The species is not affected by bronze birch borer, which is yet another reason to plant it."

Fastigiate European beech (*Fagus sylvatica* 'Fastigiata'). This upright and thinner (50-by-25-foot) cultivar of the standard European beech "shares with the species a smooth, thin bark, branching that is both straight and curvilinear, and dense, slow-to-drop foliage," says Kiely. "Photographs of specimen 'Fastigiata' depict it as tapered at the base and crown; in actuality its branches reach skyward to a crown that can be flattish and wide. Plant this cultivar in the open where the summer sky can set off its form and the winter sun its architecture and few remaining leaves."

Serbian spruce (*Picea omorika*). "Though slow growing, this dark blue, 50-by-20-foot beauty punctuates existing spruces and adds height where it is needed. Clay and loam soils accommodate it equally well and, like many spruces, this one keeps all of its slightly drooping branches over time. Salt and very strong winds are this spruce's nemeses," Kiely says.

Don't have room for a gentle giant on your property? Elisabeth Cary, education director at the Berkshire Botanical Garden, recommends the following trees and shrubs, large and small, that are hardy to Zone 5. They grow well in the botanical garden and would work for all but coldest microclimates in the northern extremes of the Berkshires. Plants accompanied by an asterisk are native to the eastern United States. Her list excludes "finicky growers," she says. "I also included plants that have some specific requirements—some grow in dry chalky soils, like the American smoke tree, while other choices can tolerate a wet setting, like black tupelo."

Large shade trees

- Sugar maple* (*Acer saccharum*)
- Shagbark hickory* (*Carya ovata*)
- Katsura tree (*Cercidiphyllum japonicum*)
- Tulip tree* (*Lirodendron tulipifera*)
- Cucumbertree magnolia* (*Magnolia acuminata*)
- Black tupelo* (*Nyssa sylvatica*)
- Bur oak* (*Quercus macrocarpa*)

Small understory flowering trees

- Shadblow or serviceberry* (*Amelanchier arborea* or *canadensis*)
- Redbud* (*Cercis canadensis*)

- White fringe tree* (*Chionanthus virginicus*)

- Pagoda dogwood* (*Cornus alternifolia*)

- American smoketree* (*Cotinus obovatus*)

- Japanese stewartia (*Stewartia pseudocamellia*)

Flowering shrubs

- Bottlebrush buckeye* (*Aesculus paviflora*)

- Alternative-leaf butterfly bush (*Buddleia alternifolia*)

- Boxwood (*Buxus microphylla*)

- Carolina allspice bush* (*Calycanthus floridus*)

- Redvein enkianthus (*Enkianthus campanulatus*)

- Bottlebrush shrub* (*Fothergilla major* 'Mount Airy')

- Witch hazel (*Hamamelis* x *intermedia* 'Arnold Promise')

- Hydrangea (*Hydrangea paniculata* 'Tardiva' and *H.* 'Pink Diamond')

- Northern bayberry* (*Myrica pensylvanicum*)

- Viburnum* (*Viburnum nudum* 'Winterthur')

On Martha's Vineyard, Nantucket, and Cape Cod, some of the best trees are stewartia, oxydendrum, American holly (*Ilex opaca*), and American species of magnolia, says Tim Boland, executive director of the Polly Hill Arboretum. Good shrubs for the Cape and Islands are Asiatic and North American azaleas, arrowwood (*Viburnum dentatum*), witherod (*Viburnum nudum*), boxwood (*Buxus*), and Winterberry (*Ilex verticillata*). For coping with the handicaps of salt-laden, seaside wind and foraging deer, David Bartsch of David Bartsch Landscape Architects on Nantucket recommends shrubs like Turkestan rose (*Rosa rugosa*), viburnum species, bayberry, white alder (*Clethra*), and groundel (*Senecio vulgaris*). For trees, he suggests Austrian pine (*Pinus nigra*), eastern red cedar (*Juniperus virginiana*), Leyland cypress (*Cupressocyparis lelylandii*), Bradford pear (*Pyrus calleryana*), Kwanzan cherry (*Prunus serrulata*), and Chinese dogwood (*Cornus kousa*).

Hedges and Screens

A hedge by definition is a collection of plants in a row, but remember that a hedge is a living plant and not a brick wall. Hedges are usually made of shrubs, but you can "hedge" trees such as beech, hornbeam, and hedge maple.

Plants have natural form; constantly pruning, clipping, and shearing a woody to the constraints of a straight hedge put it under a lot of stress, so it needs TLC. If you want a neat, formal hedge, choose plants that have a tidy habit, and be prepared to groom them twice a year.

Are you trying to enclose a vegetable garden and keep out animals? A thorny shrub may be a good choice. Do you want privacy from the neighbors? You'll want something tall that won't need a lot of fussy pruning.

Do you want evergreen or deciduous? Evergreens stay green and solid, retain a sheared shape better, and look great with a layer of snow, but they grow more slowly. Either you wait years for your hedge to fill in or you start with larger and more expensive plants. Deciduous hedges have a softer form that is gentle in summer, while in winter you notice their structure and skeleton, which many people find enormously pleasing. Plants chosen for deciduous hedges grow more quickly, and so you may spend less at the beginning. Deciduous shrubs recover from damage more quickly. They can also be pruned to the ground if necessary to renew their vigor.

Informal hedges can be planted in a loose row. Choose the more upright of the informal shrubs so that the hedge retains some structure. Rhododendrons look wonderful as a hedge. You can also create a mixed informal hedge composed of different shrubs, but take into consideration the growing conditions of each variety. Lilacs like sweet soil and azaleas prefer acidic; they might have a hard time growing well together.

When pruning a hedge, keep it slightly wider at the base than at the top to ensure that lower branches aren't shaded from the sun by branches above them.

Purchasing and Planting

You can purchase trees and shrubs in four ways:

Bare root: The plant arrives with no soil or very little soil

My Favorite Trees and Shrubs for Hedges

Formal: Beech (*Fagus*), boxwood (*Buxus*), cypress (*Chamaecyparis*), hemlock (*Tsuga*), holly (*Ilex*), juniper (*Juniperus*), ninebark (*Physocarpus*), pine (*Pinus*), spruce (*Picea*), and yew (*Taxus*).

Informal: Abelia (*Abelia*), Carolina allspice (*Calycanthus floridus*), cotoneaster (*Cotoneaster*), crab apple (*Malus*), euonymus (*Euonymus*), forsythia (*Forsythia*), hawthorn (*Crataegus*), hedge maple (*Acer campestre*), hydrangea (*Hydrangea*), hypericum (*Hypericum*), lilac (*Syringa vulgaris*), mountain laurel (*Kalmia latifolia*), plum (*Prunus*), rhododendron (*Rhododendron*), rose (*Rosa*), viburnum (*Viburnum*), willow (*Salix*), and witch hazel (*Hamamelis*).

around the roots. It will probably be packed in a plastic bag to keep roots moist.

To plant a bare-root tree, keep the roots moist right up to the time of planting. Prepare the planting hole, then create a mound in the center over which you spread the roots.

Balled and burlapped (known in the nursery trade as B&B): The plant was field grown then root pruned and its root-ball dug up with a large amount of soil. The root-ball and soil are wrapped in a fabric like burlap.

To plant a balled and burlapped tree, unwrap the root-ball and look for the trunk flare. You may need to do a little detective work and remove soil from the top of the ball to find the flare. Set the B&B plant in the hole and tip it gently to remove the twine and fabric surrounding the roots. If the wrapping is a natural burlap, you can leave the wrap in the hole because it will eventually decompose, but be careful to pull the burlap back or cut it down below soil level.

Container grown: The plant was started and grown in a pot or container.

Field grown and containerized: The plant was started in the field and then dug up and planted in a container.

To plant a container-grown or a containerized, field-grown tree, remove the plant from the container and check the roots. Are they pot bound? If the plant has been in the container too long, its roots may have started to circle around. If left this way in the planting hole, the plant will not survive. You can make several vertical slashes to loosen roots and pry them apart, spreading them around the planting hole. Or you can chop the bottom third of the root-ball off and loosen the roots. Be aware that both these practices stress the tree. The best bet is to stay away from pot-bound plants.

Plant bare-root shrubs in the late fall to early spring while the plants are dormant. Container-grown or B&B trees and shrubs can be planted any time during the growing season. If you plant in the summer, you'll need to maintain a rigorous watering schedule.

The planting rule of thumb for all woodies, whether purchased as B&B or in containers, is to prepare a hole a couple of inches shallower than the root-ball and three times its diameter. The single biggest mistake made when planting a tree or shrub is planting it too deeply. Once you've set the tree in the hole, make sure the root flare is above the soil level by about 2 inches. "Improper planting is a major cause of tree death," says Brighton garden professional Fran Gustman. "Oxygen filters downward through the soil particles to the root hairs. Carbon dioxide moves upward until it is expelled into the air." If a tree is planted too deeply, this process cannot take place correctly.

Some shallow-rooted shrubs, such as mountain laurel and rhododendrons, "can be planted quite high," adds Julie Morris, director of horticulture at Blithewold Mansion, Gardens & Arboretum in Bristol, Rhode Island. Morris emphasizes planting shrubs level with or just slightly higher than ground level—never below ground level. "You must see the flare of the plant above soil or grade level—where the trunk flares out to the roots."

Backfill the hole with the same soil that you removed, not a different soil. Experts recommend that you *not* add any soil amendments except maybe a handful of slow-release organic fertilizer. Plants should come to you in good shape and ready to survive without additional help. Tamp the backfill firmly so that the soil won't settle significantly and cause the tree to sink below grade level. Mulch well, but don't push the mulch right up against the trunk or you will encourage decay. Water the plant in its new home.

It is not recommended that you prune the tree or shrub at planting except to remove dead branches. The plant needs its leaf canopy to feed the development of new roots.

I heartily recommend bringing in a professional arborist when the tree is large. "Usually two strong people can manage a 4-inch caliper shade tree," notes Barbara Emeneau, a retired Massachusetts certified arborist in Winchester. Dr. Brian Maynard, chair of the department of plants at the University of Rhode Island, suggests people get assistance "even with a 2-inch caliper tree." A 4-inch caliper tree should have at minimum a 36-inch-wide root-ball, he says, which is very heavy. A mishandled tree can be damaged beyond recovery, even though you may not see the effects of damage for years. Professionals have the equipment to safely lift large plants.

Staking

Prevailing wisdom says that newly planted trees should not be staked unless absolutely necessary. Staking has been found to weaken trees over the long term. Left to its own devices, an unstaked tree will establish itself more quickly.

If you must stake a tree, leave the stakes in for as short a time as possible—usually one growing season. Place two stakes at equal distance from the trunk and attach them with something like polypropylene webbing, such as ArborTape, that will not damage the trunk. The webbing should not be so tight that it holds the tree rigid—it is only meant to provide backup until the tree establishes itself. Check twice a year to make sure that the webbing is not strangling the tree.

Watering

Improper irrigation is a common mistake folks make when planting a tree or a shrub. It takes a long time to wet soil, so you should water long and infrequently. Water for as much as two to three hours each time, but water slowly—a slow trickle from the hose. Water once a week for new plants and then you can ease off to every two weeks until the plant is well established. It takes time for a new plant to get established, and even a year to two after it's planted you should still be treating it like a newly installed tree. A good rule of thumb is to assume one year of establishment for each inch of trunk caliper (caliper measured at 4 feet off the ground). Thus a 2-inch caliper tree should be watered regularly for two growing seasons.

Fertilizing

The best time to fertilize a tree is about one month before root growth begins in the spring, when the soil temperature is above 50 degrees. Depending on where you live in Massachusetts, that would be about mid-March. The worst time is in late fall when the roots aren't growing—it's a waste of time and effort. And the very worst time to fertilize is mid- to late August, when the tree might respond by putting out new growth that could then freeze when the first frost hits.

Tree feeder roots are close to the surface. You can sprinkle organic fertilizer on the soil at the base of the tree working outward, or you can deep-root fertilize with injections of fertilizer toward the canopy drip line. A good topdressing of compost or manure will also benefit woodies.

Pruning

I take pruning very seriously, because so much damage can be done to a tree if pruned improperly. If you're unsure of your pruning skills, go slowly. Ask yourself if you should bring in a professional. I watched my neighbor massacre a gorgeous old cherry that had bloomed profusely every May. The result was heartbreaking.

There are two reasons for pruning. The first is aesthetic—that is, to improve the look of the tree or shrub. The second is to correct obvious problems: to remove branches that cross and rub against each other, or to remove diseased or dead limbs. I pruned my coral bark Japanese maple (*Acer palmatum* 'Sango-kaku') because it had two leaders (main stems). A tree with two leaders forming a crotch may be in danger of splitting at the crotch. I removed one of the leaders so the other could become the main trunk.

Ideally, prune trees in late winter. Insects and diseases are less active then, and as spring arrives the tree will grow and close up the wound. The worst time to prune a tree is in the fall. Trees stop growing in autumn, so wounds will remain open to winter's freezing and thawing, as well as to insects or fungal disease, until the tree resumes growth in spring.

Most flowering shrubs should be pruned in late spring or late winter, depending on the shrub's flowering schedule. Shrubs that bloom in the early spring, like azaleas, are flowering on last season's growth. Pruning them immediately after flowering gives them time to form flower buds for next year's bloomtime; prune them in winter and you lose the next year's display. Shrubs that bloom later, say June onward, generally flower on the current season's growth. Some hydrangeas, however, bloom on the second year's growth, so time your pruning accordingly.

Pruning can be done in two ways:

Topping (also called heading) means removing part of a limb, usually closer to the end of the limb. Cut back the limb to a lateral, or side, branch that is at least half the diameter of the limb being cut.

Make your pruning cut flush with the branch collar, *not* flush with the trunk. Cutting too close to the trunk is a common mistake. If the tree limb is large and heavy, make three cuts. The first cut is made furthest from the trunk; cut clean through and remove the limb. Make a second cut a bit closer to the trunk, sawing from the underside of the limb upward, and cutting only halfway through. Make the third cut flush with the collar for a clean, smooth appearance. This three-step method will prevent the entire limb from breaking off mid-prune and leaving a torn break. It is usually better to remove a whole branch rather than just prune the tips. Study the tree to determine how to achieve your goal (aesthetic or corrective) by removing whole branches back to the trunk.

Thinning means taking entire limbs out from the base of the plant or back to the trunk. When thinning to rejuvenate an old shrub, remove only one-third or one-quarter of the plant each year. It may take three to four years to rejuvenate a shrub. This is true for trees also. If you prune too much off at one time, the tree will struggle to survive.

Use the right kind of tools: clean, sharp pruning tools or saws—don't hack at a plant.

Old wisdom called for dressing pruning wounds, but this is no longer recommended because the plant can't breathe through the dressing, and moisture can collect underneath and encourage disease. The plant is better left to heal itself. Some plants like maples, birches, and yellowwood bleed when pruned in early spring, but this is more unsightly than unhealthy.

There is an art to pruning. I encourage you to stand back and look at the plant. Tie a ribbon around the limbs you are thinking of removing. Step back and imagine the plant without those branches. Will it look better? If pruning is needed for the health of the plant, then you have to make the cuts and live with the consequences. But still try to prune attractively.

Keeping Trees Healthy

There is much you can do to promote healthy tree and shrub growth: choose disease-resistant species adapted to your conditions. Plant correctly. Practice correct irrigation. Don't overfertilize. Prune in a healthy way.

Sometimes you can do everything right and still have problems, whether caused by drought, wind or sun damage, or insects and diseases. We'll talk more about some of these in chapter 10.

Diagnosing a problem is not easy. You can start by referring to horticultural reference books. You can call in a professional to look at your plant or take a good-size sample (not just one leaf) to your local garden center. You can call the Massachusetts Horticultural Society HortLine (617–933–4929) for advice and for the date of their next plant clinic. Treat your gentle giants with the TLC they deserve.

Top Trees

These are my favorite trees and shrubs that grow at the Arnold Arboretum in Jamaica Plain.

- Hedge maple (*Acer campestre*)
- Paperbark maple (*Acer griseum*)
- Striped maple (*Acer pensylvanicum*)
- Katsura tree (*Cercidiphyllum japonicum*)
- Yellowwood (*Cladrastis kentuckea*)
- Kousa dogwood (*Cornus kousa*)
- European beech (*Fagus sylvatica*)
- Ginkgo (*Ginkgo biloba*)
- Winterberry (*Ilex verticillata*)
- Goldenraintree (*Koelreuteria paniculata*)
- Star magnolia (*Magnolia stellata*)
- Japanese umbrella pine (*Sciadoppitys verticillata*)
- Japanese pagoda tree (*Styphnolobium japonicum*)
- Japanese tree lilac (*Syringa reticulata*)
- Common lilac (*Syringa vulgaris*)
- Koreanspice viburnum (*Viburnum carlesii*)

Trees play an important role in my gardening life because of their quiet beauty, enduring quality, strength, and grace. I planted a hedge maple (*Acer campestre*) at Blithewold in memory of my mother, and I am waiting for the perfect tree to plant nearby in memory of my father. Trees evoke awe, respect, admiration—and a great quietude.

CHAPTER EIGHT

Lawn

Cold winters and humid summers put hefty demands on Massachusetts turfgrass. The adage "The right plant in the right place" is every bit as relevant for grass as for any other growing thing. That carpet of green you see before you is made up of individual plants—about a million plants per 1,000 square feet, writes Stuart Franklin in his book *Building a Healthy Lawn*. The key is growing the right grass variety for the climate—and then giving it appropriate care.

Lawns do more than just look pretty. "Lawns cool the air by releasing oxygen, they help control pollution and reduce soil erosion, and they purify and replenish our water supply," explains James Novak, director of public information at the nonprofit Turf

The Living Lawn

For a look at a beautiful demonstration lawn, I urge you to visit the Living Lawn Project in Marblehead. Begun in August 1998 in response to home owners' demands for information on nontoxic lawn care programs, co-creators Patricia Beckett and Chip Osborne initially used any kind of seed they could get donated. They now favor the one mix they found does better than others: North Country Organics Eco-Blend. At the project's Web site (www.livinglawn.org), you can download a free brochure, *Simple Steps Towards a Healthy Lawn*, or make a donation to the project.

Resource Center. On a hot summer day, Novak says, lawns will be 30 degrees cooler than asphalt and 14 degrees cooler than bare soil. "The front lawns of eight houses have the cooling effect of about seventy tons of air-conditioning. That's amazing, considering the average home has an air conditioner with just a three- or four-ton capacity."

Massachusetts Grass

Turfgrasses are divided into warm- and cool-weather species. Cool-weather grasses grow better in spring and fall and best suit the Massachusetts climate. When temperatures rise in summer, cool-seaon grasses go dormant and turn brown, returning to green when the heat diminishes. Warm-weather grasses are brown in spring and fall but green up in the dog days of summer.

Turfgrass has two growing habits: 1) sod-forming grass that spreads by stolons (stems that travel just above the soil surface) or rhizomes (stems that travel under the soil surface) and 2) bunching or clumping grass that spreads from tillers (new shoots that form at the base of the plant).

Cool-Season Grasses

These cool-season grasses are recommended by the Massachusetts Department of Food and Agriculture. You can download their copyright-free manual *A Homeowner's Guide to Environmentally Sound Lawncare* at www.mass.gov.

- Kentucky bluegrass
- Annual ryegrass
- Perennial ryegrass
- Tall fescue
- Creeping red fescue
- Hard fescue
- Chewings fescue
- Red fescue

There is a turf to meet every need, depending on your site, your soil, and your requirements for that lawn. Will the grass get high or low traffic—family football games or a quiet reading area? Is it in sun or shade, or a combination? Does your lawn need to cope with salt-laden water and desiccating winds, as on the Islands and the Cape? Do you want perfectly manicured green or a looser, more free-range look?

The staple New England grass, according to James Novak of the Turf Resource Center, is 100 percent bluegrass. A hardy turf that tends to thrive in the New England climate, bluegrass spreads by rhizomes, which enables it to create a smooth, carpetlike appearance. For lawns constantly trampled by active kids, you might add in perennial ryegrass. It's the only major cool-season grass that "combines both superior wear and compaction tolerance," according to the National Turfgrass Evaluation Program. "Mixtures of bluegrass and ryegrass provide sports turf with all the qualities critical for turf that's subject to heavy traffic." In contrast, a yard used only for weekend barbecues and get-togethers won't necessarily need a high-traffic blend.

Many experts recommend using a blend of grass varieties. Different grasses have different degrees of adaptability to sun or shade and dampness or dryness as well as amount of disease or grub resistance. Horticulturist and landscape designer Michael

Talbot in Mashpee recommends fescues wherever cool-season grasses are needed—"preferably a blend of improved cultivars of hard fescue, creeping red fescue, and chewings fescue, with 10 percent bluegrass." He includes a higher percentage of bluegrass in sunny areas with very good soils and mild summers.

"I use blends because I think one variety will do better in each microenvironment of a yard," says Mike Murray of Organic Soil Solutions in Woburn. "And certain qualities of the various grasses complement each other." Murray specializes in installing and maintaining organic lawns. He uses a blend created at the University of Rhode Island that contains a lot of tall fescue.

On the Cape and Islands, where it is warmer but where the soils are poor, droughty, and acidic, Talbot recommends including 20 to 30 percent of an improved tall fescue turfgrass to the mix. Improved tall fescue is a very adaptable, tough, drought- and shade-tolerant turfgrass that even tolerates some soil salinity.

But even warm-season grasses may have a place in Massachusetts. They work well for folks who are Bay State residents only in the summer months. "If green grass is not so important to you through the spring and fall but you want green grass in the hot, dry summer months only, then you may want to choose warm-season grasses like buffalo grass or bermuda grass," says Paul Sachs of North Country Organics in Vermont.

Turfgrasses are annual or perennial: There is both an annual and a perennial ryegrass, for instance. The annual grasses germinate quickly, the perennial more slowly. And different varieties germinate at different times: Bluegrass germinates in about a month, and tall fescue in three weeks or less. A mix of grasses will give you a combination of grasses that come up more quickly and shade the grasses that are germinating more slowly.

Make sure the label indicates exactly what seeds are in the bag. Choose a quality seed—some cheap mixes contain a lot of filler or the wrong type of grass for your conditions. And check the date. Old seed may not germinate consistently. There are countless blends. North Country Organics, for example, offers about a dozen blends for different situations, some with clover and some without, some for shade, for grub control, for full sun, for drought. Their Eco-Blend, for instance, contains (in descending order) tall fescue, chewings fescue, perennial ryegrass, hard fescue, Kentucky bluegrass, red fescue, redtop, and white clover. They also offer an Eco-Blend without clover. Clover, far from being a weed, can add nitrogen to the soil. "Much to the chagrin of some turf experts," clover is an excellent additive to grass seed, says Western Massachusetts master gardener Nancy Howell. "It adds texture and remains green long after most grasses turn brown."

The same rules for selecting seed apply to sod. Know what grasses have been used to create the sod you are buying and buy from a reputable turf supplier. Many turfgrass sod producers in the New England area grow blends of bluegrass, fine fescue, bentgrass, ryegrass, and other varieties, says James Novak of the Turf Resource Center.

Seeding or Sodding a Lawn

You can use seed or sod to create a new lawn or repair an existing lawn. Either way, the single most important thing to do is to prepare the soil. Rich soil will provide the plant with nutrients to build a strong root system, from which leaf blades in turn get their water and nutrients.

I recommend beginning with a soil test (see chapter 1) to determine what kind of lawn soil you have, what condition it's in, and if (or how much) the pH needs to be raised or lowered. Turfgrass grows best in a soil with a pH of 6.2 to 6.8.

Incorporate 3 to 4 inches of good loam into the existing soil. You can add amendments at this time if the soil test calls for them—things such as lime, compost, manure, and a slow-release fertilizer rich in phosphorus (like bonemeal or rock phosphate). Till well and leave the soil loose, free of large stones, and raked smooth. You can fertilize more in the spring, when the grass is well established, with a fertilizer rich in nitrogen, such as cotton-seed meal or dried blood.

Seed

How much seed will you need? The rule of thumb is three million seeds per 1,000 square feet. There are about two million seeds in a pound of bluegrass; about 250,000 seeds in a pound of tall fescue. The label on the seed bag should indicate the square footage that bag covers.

Start seeding or laying sod in late August to early September. Temperatures are not too hot and the plants have a chance to get established and strong before cold weather hits.

Broadcast the seed evenly over the area and press the seeds in lightly. Rolling a large garbage can over the area will help with this. Then water well. Keep it well watered. Keep the area moist but not soaking wet until the seeds germinate. Once-a-day watering will suffice unless it rains or the sun is not shining. Continue to water frequently to keep moist, but it is possible to rot the seeds if you give them too much water, so monitor the moisture of the soil. Once the seeds have germinated (which may take a couple of weeks or up to a month) ease off on the watering, but still keeping the new turf evenly moist. And treat the area gently. Maybe rope it off so that people don't walk on it. Give the area time to get established and go gently with the first mowing. Remember these are new young seedlings, and lawn mowers are heavy machines.

Starting a new lawn on a slope may require more scrupulous attention to grading, seeding, and watering to ensure seeds get spread evenly and do not get washed away. Watering evenly may be a little tricky too, so monitor the distribution of water to see how much gets dispersed to the different areas. (See details on watering in chapter 3.)

Sod

Sod usually comes in strips 6 feet long by 18 inches wide that are laid with staggered joints, like a brick walkway, so that the strips knit together seamlessly. The best time to place sod is in late summer and in fall. Sod should be laid within twenty-four hours of being harvested; when ordering sod make sure the site is prepared and ready to accept the strips. Sod left in a pile will heat up, cook, and die. If you can't lay the sod that very day, water the pile and cover it to keep it moist. Sod that dries out typically will not come back, whereas seed will go dormant and recover when watered or the rains return.

Once applied, water the sod immediately, and water daily for the first three weeks, then frequently after that. Within a month the lawn should be well on its way to being rooted in. Don't water if it rains and don't overwater.

Depending on the growing conditions, you can mow the sod for the first time ten to fourteen days after laying it. Let the soil dry out a little bit before the first mowing so that the mower doesn't push down on the grass. This applies to a seeded lawn also.

Maintaining a Lawn

A lawn needs water, nutrients, air, sunlight, and regular cutting to keep it healthy—and a healthy lawn experiences fewer disease and pest problems.

Watering: In general, apply 1 inch of water a week. Turfgrass in full sun may need more water than turf in the shade, so monitor how deeply the water penetrates the soil (see chapter 3). Regular, deep watering helps establish a deep, drought-resistant root system.

Mowing: "The one thing people do wrong over and over is scalping their lawn—mowing very short. This opens it up to crabgrass germination," says Patricia Beckett, a land-care professional accredited by the Northeast Organic Farming Association. During the growing season, "mow high—3 inches or higher—to protect your grass from drought and stress and to shade weeds." Adds Mike Murray of Woburn: "Higher mowing also provides more grass blade leaf surface so sunlight is more readily absorbed, helping with photosynthesis." A higher cut also improves appearance because it looks thicker from a distance, blemishes are less noticeable, and the grass has a deeper root system. But don't wait until the lawn is *too* long, or the grass blades will fall over, making it harder to get a good cut. You can lower the mowing height when growth slows down as the grass approaches dormancy.

Experts recommend only taking off one-third of the leaf blade at one mowing. Keep your mower blades sharp. Dull blades tear the leaf blade, and that "creates a larger surface area which serves as a port of entry for disease organisms," states Bruce Wenning, horticulturist and grounds manager for the Massachusetts Audubon Society's Habitat Wildlife Sanctuary. "Tearing calls on the roots for more carbohydrate reserves for wound healing, thereby weakening the turf."

All lawn experts seem to agree that people should leave the grass clippings on the lawn, unless the clippings are very long.

Grass clippings are 80 percent water. They decompose quickly and recycle nutrients, particularly nitrogen, back into the soil.

Fertilizing: Grass plants grow in the spring, using the nutrients stored in the roots from the previous fall. In Massachusetts it makes sense to fertilize in early fall, when the grass comes out of summer dormancy. Fertilize again in mid-fall, when growth slows down, so the turfgrass can store nutrients again for the following year. Some folks like to fertilize around Memorial Day, and while this certainly won't harm your lawn, it isn't the optimum time.

Know your soil and its needs. A light topdressing with a high quality compost, manure, or slow-release fertilizer is an excellent way to boost the soil. In general, though, what lawns need most are lime and nitrogen. Lime raises the pH level of the soil to make it less acidic. Grass grows best at a pH of 6.2 to 6.8. But don't throw lime on your lawn unless you need it! Your soil test will indicate your lawn's pH and how much (if any) lime is needed. The normal recommendation is fifty to one hundred pounds of lime per 1,000 square feet applied every two years. The most common source of lime is dolomitic lime.

Wait a week after applying lime before fertilizing. Fertilize just before a good rain or water in the fertilizer so that it doesn't sit on top of the lawn.

Bonemeal can be a useful fertilizer. It raises the soil pH as it helps the grass develop strong root systems the first season, according to landscape designer and horticulturist Kathryn Haigh, owner of Seaside Gardens on Nantucket. "I am not sure if I would recommend this to home owners with dogs, though, as dogs love to dig at the bonemeal!" she laughs.

Peter Coppola, a Massachusetts Horticultural Society master gardener in Burlington, favors a dilute ammonia solution to get nitrogen onto his lawn. "Household ammonia contains ammonium hydroxide and has an N-P-K of 17-0-0. Since the whole idea is to get the grass up quickly and prevent weed seeds from germinating, I spray every week."

Green and Healthy

Pests, weeds, and diseases are indications of poor soil. A weak lawn is an invitation to pests and diseases. But don't whip yourself into a frenzy (like I did!) if you notice ugly rings in the grass or see birds pecking at the grubs in your lawn—identify the problem and get advice on how to deal with it.

Lawn Pests

Sod webworms, chinch bugs, moles, and grubs are frequently pests in Massachusetts lawns. Of these, the most common pests are grubs—specifically Japanese beetle (*Popillia japonica*), Oriental beetle (*Anomala orientalis*), European chafer (*Rhizotrogus majalis*), and Asiatic garden beetle (*Maladera castanea*), according to Bruce Wenning at the Massachusetts Audubon Society's Habitat Wildlife Sanctuary. "Lawns that are attacked by these pests show poor vigor, thin turf, smaller to no roots, and bare spots susceptible to weed colonization," he says.

"Many home owners and landscapers battle white grubs without much success because they assume that all white grubs are the Japanese beetle," Wenning adds. "They are not!" Properly identify your grub, and you can select the right method to control them. Some controls include:

Nematodes are microscopic worms that attack insects. The nematode *Heterorhabditis bacteriophora* is an effective biocontrol against Japanese beetle grubs; the nematode *Steinernema carpocapsae* is not. The correct nematodes will work on sod webworms and chinch bugs also. "Commercially available nematodes are specific to pests stated on the label," Wenning says. "For best results, read and follow all labeled instructions and be certain that the beneficial nematode matches the biology of the pest in question."

Milky disease (*Bacillus popillae*) contains natural bacteria that infect and kill certain species of grubs. Sold commercially as Milky Spore, the bacteria are applied to the soil, where they remain for many years, to continue infecting future generations of grubs.

Another "pest" is the family dog. Dog urine is high in nitrogen and can burn the lawn. Rake out the dead grass and overseed those spots in the fall to repair the damage.

Weeds

Healthy grass is vigorous and will crowd out weeds. Weeds like poor soils, so thwart their efforts by improving your soil. Bare spots in a lawn are an open invitation to weeds. I once had a children's trampoline in the lawn for several years. When I removed it, there was a bare spot. I didn't get around to reseeding that spot when I should have, so it turned into a huge circle of weeds in the middle of my lawn—a bad fairy ring.

Identify the weeds you have in your lawn, and don't let them go to seed. Weeds can be annual or perennial, grassy or broadleaved. Perennial weeds are hardest to eliminate. At the very least, mow weeds down before they flower. You'll find a list of problem weeds and the correct treatment in chapter 10.

Corn gluten meal has received a lot of press as a weed supressant. It stops root formation as a plant germinates. It is also rich in nitrogen, which improves the soil.

Commercial "weed-killer" products are on the market, made from horticultural oils and fatty acids, but strengthening the soil and therefore the plants is the best way of dealing with weeds.

David Mellor, the groundskeeper at Fenway Park, looks after

the most famous grass in the state and one that is on show much of the time. He recently published *The Lawn Bible*, an excellent read for lawn enthusiasts. In it he recommends overseeding to repair areas that are bare or damaged and to thicken the lawn: "Healthy grass will crowd out weeds," he says. Overseed cool-season grasses at the same time of year as you would when seeding a new lawn—in the fall.

Horticulturist Kathryn Haigh agrees: "Overseeding in the spring and fall seems to keep the weeds from starting in the gaps, particularly in sun-shade lawns." Haigh has used seed mixes of sun- and shade-loving grasses, but she finds these mixed-light lawns tend to be more difficult to care for since they are often under trees. "They can be easily over- or underwatered and don't seem to develop deep root systems," she adds.

Paul Tukey, publisher and editor of *People, Places & Plants* and a founder of www.SafeLawns.org, writes in his book *The Organic Lawn Care Manual* that he encourages folks to accept a few weeds as a part of a natural environment. "I would encourage a high tolerance for some weeds, as they come and go," he adds.

Thatch

Thatch is not caused by leaving lawn clippings on the lawn. It is caused primarily by poor lawn care—heavy nitrogen fertilizer applications, watering frequently but lightly, and mowing too short. The result is a build-up of dead and dying grass stems and roots that settle on the soil surface and do not decompose properly. Soil becomes compacted, water does not drain through, and roots reach up to get the water. You end up with an impenetrable mat. A thick layer of thatch creates an environment for disease and pests and can also hamper mowing at the correct height.

Thatch takes years to accumulate. To remove it, aerate the lawn with a core aerator, a piece of machinery that pulls up 2- to 3-inch-deep plugs of soil from the lawn. You can leave the plugs on top of the lawn, like clippings, and they will break down.

Aeration opens up the lawn, aiding in water and fertilizer penetration and earthworm activity and thus starting the thatch-decomposition process. You can speed the process by using a thatching rake when the mat becomes workable. The best times to aerate are spring and fall, when grass is growing and not dormant.

Diseases

Diseases attack a lawn because the lawn is susceptible to attack. The single best way to prevent disease is to build a strong lawn and water correctly, in the morning if possible. Choosing disease-resistant varieties of grass will go a long way toward preventing diseases from taking hold. But if you do have a diseased lawn, you should first identify the problem correctly.

For garden professional Betsy Williams in Andover, turf is all about balance: "The secret is that my green lawn isn't just grass," she says. "It is a thick, healthy mix of grass, clover, dandelions,

---

Lawn Diseases

These diseases are listed by the Massachusetts Department of Food and Agriculture. Lawn diseases often show up as circular spots in the lawn, and these diseases look the same to the untrained eye. Have a professional diagnose your problem and recommend treatment.

Summer patch: A smoke-colored ring caused by a fungus

Fusarium blight: Light brown dead spots on the leaf blades

Leaf spot: White cottony strands near the edge of the dead spot

Snow mold: Irregularly shaped patches of tan or rusty brown

Dollar spot: Light brown dead spots on the leaf blades

Powdery mildew: White powdery covering on the leaf blades

Red thread: Rust-colored dead patches

---

ajuga, violets, alehoof, veronica, and a few other old friends. It is a true herbal lawn, and it works."

Western Massachusetts master gardener Nancy Howell likes to tell people that it's okay to have a less-than-perfect lawn. The Western Massachusetts Master Gardener Association recommends that gardeners reconsider the role of lawn. "We hope to change attitudes over time, so that people might consider lawns as the palette on which to create gardens or areas for trees and shrubs."

It really is all about balance.

CHAPTER NINE

Invasive Plants

In the nearly thirty years that I've been writing, I've learned a great deal about diverse subjects. Since becoming a master gardener and pursuing the Royal Horticultural Society's certificate in horticulture, I have learned *and* become passionate about the topic of invasive plants.

I started my gardening life in complete ignorance of the dangers of invasives. Full of my own skills as a new gardener, I happily planted Japanese honeysuckle (*Lonicera japonica*) and porcelain berry vine (*Ampelopsis brevipedunculata*). Then my friend Amy Wright, a naturalist and botanical illustrator, scolded me and explained why these plants were problems. Thankfully, both plants failed to take hold. I felt like I'd been given a second chance.

Invasive plants are "nonnative species that have spread into native or minimally managed plant systems in Massachusetts," according to the Massachusetts Invasive Plant Advisory Group (MIPAG). "These plants cause economic or environmental harm by developing self-sustaining populations and becoming dominant and/or disruptive to those systems."

To earn the label "invasive," a plant "must be able to compete aggressively and to the exclusion of native species," writes natural resources specialist Thomas Kyker-Snowman in *Downstream*, the newsletter of the Massachusetts Department of

Conservation and Recreation Division of Watershed Management. "The worst of the invaders are displacing entire associations of native species and replacing them with alien monocultures." An alarming number of species do extremely well in the wild because they often have arrived in the United States without bringing along the pests that eat them, he says.

A plant may be invasive in one area of the country and not in another. Butterfly bush (*Buddleia davidii*), for instance, is invasive in the South but not in New England. But other invasives—such as purple loosestrife (*Lythrum salicaria*)—have spread across the continent.

Not every plant that we gardeners call "aggressive" or "a thug" is technically an invasive species. "Just because a plant is a thug in the garden does not make it an invasive species in the wild," says William Brumback, conservation director for the New England Wild Flower Society. He adds, however, that thuggish behavior should send up a warning to watch for invasion into the wild. For instance, one bully that is not technically an "invasive" but is aggressive for me and many others is gooseneck loosestrife (*Lysimachia clethroides*), with roots that snake insidiously under the soil and send shoots up everywhere, until the entire perennial bed is filled with white goosenecks swaying in the breeze.

The Massachusetts Prohibited Plant List

People call the list of invasive plants the Rogue's Gallery, but I like to think of it as the Gallery of Bullies—"rogue" has too cheerful a connotation. Nearly 150 species are identified as invasive in Massachusetts. The New England Wild Flower Society, in conjunction with the Massachusetts Invasive Plant Advisory Group, published a list of sixty-six critical offenders, and in 2005 the Department of Agricultural Resources took all sixty-six plants from the MIPAG list and made it illegal to import or sell them in Massachusetts. The law took effect in January 2006, with some exceptions for mostly ornamental species like burning bush and Norway maple, which had a final import date of July 2006 and final sale dates of either January 2007 or January 2009. After these dates, gardeners will no longer be able to purchase these plants in Massachusetts.

Invasives are opportunists. They can handle tough growing conditions and spread rapidly. Their seeds can be dispersed by

Oh So Common, Oh So Invasive

Here are a choice few of the most invasive plants in Massachusetts. For the full list of all 141 species, visit www.mass.gov/agr/farmproducts/proposed_prohibited _plant_list_v12-12-05.htm. You'll find extensive additional resources about invasive plants in chapter 12.

- Oriental bittersweet (*Celastrus orbiculatus*)
- Purple loosestrife (*Lythrum salicaria*)
- Autumn olive (*Elaeagnus umbella*)
- Japanese honeysuckle (*Lonicera japonica*)
- Multiflora rose (*Rosa multiflora*)
- Garlic mustard (*Alliaria petiolata*)
- Common buckthorn (*Rhamnus cathartica*)
- Japanese barberry (*Berberis thumbergii*)
- Common barberry (*Berberis vulgaris*)
- Japanese knotweed (*Polygonum cuspidatum*)
- Norway maple (*Acer platanoides*)
- Goutweed (*Aegopodium podagraria*)

Some aquatic invasives include:

- Common reed (*Phragmites australis*)
- Eurasian water milfoil (*Myriophyllus spicatum*)
- Purple loosestrife is also listed as an aquatic invasive by the Massachusetts Office of Coastal Zone Management.

birds, wind, or water; on the fur of animals; and in the tread of car tires. The statistics about the problem of invasive plants are staggering. Consider these facts:

- Invasives now infest more than 100,000,000 acres of land in the United States.

- Our natural habitats on public land are being lost at the rate of 4,600 acres a day to invasive species.

- Of the 235 woody plants known to invade natural areas in the United States, 85 percent were introduced primarily for ornamental and landscape purposes and another 14 percent for agricultural uses.

- Purple loosestrife now grows in forty-eight states and costs $45 million per year in control and forage loss.

- Massachusetts state agencies spent over half a million dollars in 2001 on the control of nonindigenous aquatic plants.

"Many ecologists now feel that invasive species represent the greatest current and future threat to native plant and animal species worldwide—greater even than human population growth, land development, and pollution," writes William Cullina, nursery manager of the New England Wild Flower Society and author of three books. When he spoke in 2006 about invasive plants at the green industry convention New England Grows, he noted that "there are almost 3,000 species of plants growing wild in Massachusetts, and about half have been introduced either on purpose or by accident from around the world."

When invasives bully their way into an environment, they change the ecosystem—and biodiversity is lost. Soils change as plants like autumn olive contribute to an overabundance of nitrogen in the soil, which throws soil makeup out of balance. Too much nitrogen will cause plants to grow primarily foliage and no blooms. Aquatic invasive plants like fanwort (*Cabomba caroliniana*) and waterweed (*Egeria densa*) choke the waterways and change the chemistry of Bay State water. Animal habitats are

altered if not lost to certain animals entirely. When the native
plants are choked out, birds and
insects lose food sources. Take the
monarch butterfly as one example. When it
"lays its eggs on the invasive black swallowwort (*Cynanchum nigrum*) rather than on the close
kin native milkweed (*Asclepias*), the larvae die when
they hatch and try to feed on swallowwort," states scientist and
environmentalist Lisa Lofland Gould, founder of the Rhode Island
Wild Plant Society.

An area can eventually become inhospitable to anything that
does not support that particular invasive plant.

Your Choice Matters

If invasives are such a widespread problem, what can we, as gardeners, do? First, look close to home. Do you grow any plants that
are on the state invasive species list? Many of us planted orna-

mental invasives years ago, not knowing better. I was sad to see that one of my garden plants, the yellow iris (*Iris pseudocarus*) is on the list. And this is just one garden—multiply that by all the gardens in my neighborhood and extrapolate further—think of what these invasive plants are doing to every garden, botanical garden, wetland, and natural area. You start to comprehend the enormity of the problem.

Nancy Howell, a Western Massachusetts master gardener, thinks the subject of invasive plants needs a great deal more PR: "Martha Stewart, up until recently, used bittersweet in arrangements. How can we overcome that way of thinking?"

It's been hard to give up my porcelain berry vine (*Ampelopsis*), but I accepted that it had been ruled invasive and saw an opportunity to experiment with something new. I replaced the porcelain berry with a golden hop vine (*Humulus lupulus* 'Aureus'), which is great fun.

Eradicate the Invaders

Betsy Williams of the Proper Season in Andover continually combats one invasive that has all but taken over her garden—oriental bittersweet (*Celastrus orbiculatus*). She has been digging, pulling, and burning young bittersweet vines out of every bed, bush, and border on her property since she bought it. "We try to keep it cut, mowed, and yanked, but it still is a problem."

Once invasives are entrenched, it takes a multistep approach to remove them:

Hand pulling. To get rid of barberry, euonymus, and honeysuckle, Western Massachusetts master gardener Mary-Jane Emmet of Lenox digs, digs, digs. Brian Duncan, a Massachusetts Horticultural Society master gardener in Methuen, has fought with his invasive plants for more than eight years. "Keeping ahead of invasives without using chemical controls is almost a part-time job. The trick is ensuring that the invasives are removed

early, especially young Japanese barberry, multiflora rose, and Japanese knotweed volunteers," he says.

Establishing barriers. Duncan recently discovered that using pieces of sod was "somewhat effective" in slowing down established clumps of Japanese knotweed. In Nantucket, landscape designer and horticulturist Kathryn Haigh of Seaside Gardens battles Japanese knotweed with berms of topsoil covered with heavy-duty landscape fabric, with mixed results. She is considering ordering thick plastic barriers with patented locks, normally used to control bamboos, to keep the neighboring knotweed off her property.

Repeated mowing. In the summer Mary-Jane Emmet just keeps mowing the Japanese knotweed down to the ground to weaken the plants. "A golf course professional I know calls this 'carbohydrate starvation,'" she says.

Biological controls. Certain insects are known to feed on problem plants. Research is currently being conducted on two species of leaf beetle (*Galerucella calmariensis* and *G. pusilla*) that have been found to feed on the invasive purple loosestrife. Tim Simmons, restoration ecologist with the Massachusetts Heritage and Endangered Species Program (www.nhesp.org), said they have "embraced this beetle" wholeheartedly. He visited one site recently where the loosestrife was not just reduced, it was gone! Learn more about the success of this biological control online at the University of Connecticut (www.ladybug.uconn.edu) or Cornell University (www.gardening.cornell.edu).

Chemical controls. You may not need to pull out the big herbicide guns to slow down and stop invasives. Duncan has found that if he cuts Japanese knotweed down to about 6 inches in the spring and pours table salt and horticultural-grade vinegar (more than 20 percent stronger than table vinegar) into the hollow stems, the plant struggles for a year or two and eventually expires. But, he says, "it is still a never-ending battle."

Many experts who would never normally advocate using chemicals do, in fact, say that sometimes the invasive is worse than the chemical. But not all chemical herbicides work on all plants and different herbicides work on different plants. It is essential that you know exactly what plant you are trying to eradicate and what

Stop the Invaders!

- Avoid planting nonnative species that are known to be invasive.
- Encourage nurseries to stop selling these plants.
- Do not dig up native plants from the wild to transplant to your own garden—this leaves holes in the natural space, and invasives are opportunists that will fill in those holes.
- Plant more native species—there are plenty of beautiful ones.
- Encourage legislators to create more stringent bans on the importation of nonnative invasives.
- Educate yourself and those you know about the dangers of invasive plants. Spread the word!

chemical will work on it. And note that there is a correct and incorrect time of year to apply herbicides to specific plants.

Using herbicides on wetlands is highly regulated by the state—you can't spritz that purple loosestrife growing alongside the stream on your property without a state permit (see www.mass.gov/dep/water/approvals/wm04app.doc). The herbicide Rodeo, a version of Round-up manufactured for controlled use in wetlands, will kill or cripple every photosynthesizing thing it touches. It must be applied by an experienced person with a state license to use herbicides. You can contact the Department of Conservation & Recreation's Office of Watershed Management (617–626–1379; www.mass.gov./dcr/) or your local conservation commission to find someone certified to apply herbicides within wetlands.

Proper disposal. Do not put invasive plants on the compost heap. Plants like knotweed can root easily from cuttings, and most compost piles are not hot enough to kill seeds. Some folks put plant debris in a plastic bag and leave it to cook in the sun. The downside of this is that it can take a couple of months for the debris to decompose, and you're never entirely sure if the weeds and seeds have totally cooked. I simply recommend taking the debris to the dump. If you want to burn your debris, check with your local fire department to see if you need a permit. Definitely do not burn poison ivy—the smoke can be toxic.

Elegant Substitutes

The best substitutes for alien invasives are tried-and-true native plants. I think there's a tendency to think that "all native" will mean "all the same" and "boring." But this is not true. "Folks just don't realize how many alternatives are available," says Debra Strick of the New England Wild Flower Society. "We have over 1,500 beautiful native species here at Garden in the Woods, both planted and for sale."

Here are some beautiful alternatives to common invasive plants:

Autumn olive: Replace with highbush cranberry (*Viburnum trilobum*) or winterberry (*Ilex verticillata*).

Burning bush: Replace with bayberry (*Myrica pensylvanica*) or red chokeberry (*Aronia arbutifolia*).

Purple loosestrife: Replace with swamp milkweed (*Asclepias incarnata*) or blue giant hyssop (*Agastache foeniculum*).

Of the many other native plants that can be used as replacements, laurel (*Kalmia*), winterberry (*Ilex verticillata*), fothergilla, dogwood (*Cornus*), sweetshrub (*Calycanthus*), viburnum, and hydrangea are just a few. Visit the New England Wild Flower Society's Web site (www.newfs.org) for a full list titled "Native Alternatives for Invasive Ornamental Plant Species." This list also appears in William Cullina's book *Native Trees, Shrubs & Vines*, a wonderful read on natives.

"Instead of searching for a few species that will grow anywhere—idiot-proof plants, if you will—we, as gardeners and landscape professionals, need to broaden our horizons quite a bit," says Cullina. "We have an amazing native flora here, which can fill our gardens and wild lands with beauty, diversity, and life if we just take the time to notice and learn."

How can you argue with that?

Garden
Solutions

Coping
with Pests and
Diseases

Having healthy plants is all about keeping an eye on the whole picture. Plants don't have problems in isolation. A plant disease develops when three factors are present: First, a susceptible plant. Plants that are stressed are more vulnerable to attack. Second, there must be a pathogen: a disease-causing fungus, bacterium, or virus. Third, environmental conditions must favor development of the pathogen. This three-part process is known as the disease triangle. Remove just one of the three factors and disease will not develop.

That's where integrated pest management—IPM—comes in. You may be familiar with this concept, or with IDM, integrated disease management (the latter a term used primarily by the nursery industry). IPM and IDM are techniques for solving the problems of disease and pest damage in a more holistic and ecologically friendly way, with an emphasis on using the least toxic approach. In this chapter I'm going to use the term IPM to refer to both techniques. We'll look at IPM in general terms first, and then we'll talk about specific garden pest problems and what you can do about them.

Integrated Pest Management

Integrated pest management is a commonsense, environmentally friendly approach to controlling garden pests. IPM uses a combination of pest-control tactics: cultural, physical and mechanical, biological, and chemical. You start with the most environmentally friendly tactic and resort to natural or chemical pesticides only if other methods fail. The idea is to find natural ways to reduce pests and decrease the use of chemicals.

"One common misconception is that IPM involves the control of insects only," says Brian Duncan, a Massachusetts Horticultural Society master gardener in Methuen. In actuality, weeds and diseases fit the IPM definition of pest.

When you practice IPM, you tailor your strategy to each pest. There is no one-size-fits-all solution. In each case your choices are based on approaches suited for the plants you're growing (fruit, vegetables, shrubs, flowers), the pest, and your location, according to the USDA Natural Resources Conservation Service. There are many variations on the IPM approach, but they all share these key steps:

1. Identify the problem correctly. The first thing is to know what the healthy plant looks like. I once saw an agave that I thought was diseased because it was covered in brown spots. Then I saw the plant name, *Agave virginica* 'Spot', and realized the spots were normal. Knowing a plant's normal, healthy appearance and growth habit will help you recognize when something is wrong.

Be a plant sleuth. Create a case history for the sick plant. What symptoms does it display—wilted or yellowed leaves? Holes in the leaves? Is the problem just on one part of the plant, on new or old leaves, or everywhere? Was the plant healthy when you first obtained it? What are the conditions the plant is growing in? What is the soil like? What is the sun exposure? How much water does it get? Are there sick plants nearby?

Consider these plant problems and their typical symptoms:

- Fungal diseases: Rot, decay, and mold are indications of fungal disease. The entire plant may be shriveled, discolored, and misshapen. Mold can look like a dusting of gray, black, or white flour. There's often a look of soft wateriness to the plants.

- Bacterial diseases: The plant may smell bad, the leaves may be yellowed, curled, stunted, and spotty. Fruits and roots may have soft slimy areas, flowers may be dried up, and stems may be blackened or wilted with wartlike growths.

- Viral diseases: The entire plant may be stunted in growth and misshapen, with yellowing leaves that are mottled and curling with no visible veins.

- Insect pests: Leaves, fruit, stems, and roots may exhibit chew marks or holes. Leaves may drop off. Tiny eggs may be attached to the upper or lower sides of leaves. Flowers, fruits, and roots may be malformed or underdeveloped.

- Environmental factors (drought, road salt damage, overwatering): The edges of the leaves may turn brown and they may drop. The leaves may be irregularly bleached or mottled.

- Nutrient deficiencies can mimic the damage caused by disease. For example, lack of nitrogen may cause leaves to lose some color and turn yellowish; a potassium deficiency may cause leaves to turn grayish green.

2. Identify the pest. This is admittedly the tough part—the time when you turn to books, online fact sheets, or experts. My favorite resources are *Mac's Field Guide,* a laminated sheet showing good and bag bugs for the Northeast; *Garden Insects of North America: The Ultimate Guide to Backyard Bugs; Weeds of the Northeast;* and *The Organic Gardener's Home Reference: A Plant-by-Plant Guide to Growing Fresh, Healthy Food.* Talk to an expert at the neighborhood garden center or master gardener hotline (see the "Hotline Help" sidebar). You might want to get a copy of *Insect and Mite Pests of Shade Trees and Woody Ornamentals* written by entomologists Robert Childs and Jennifer Konieczny for UMass Extension's Landscape, Nursery and Urban Forestry Program (see chapter 12). Although this was written for professional use, it includes more than a dozen handy checklists that detail when pests are active, and it lists insects and mites by host plant and type of injury.

Remember: Until you know the exact cause of the problem, you won't be able to select the right treatment for the pest.

Hotline Help

- Massachusetts Horticultural Society HortLine. Operates Monday, Wednesday, and Friday 10:00 A.M. to 2:00 P.M. year-round; Saturday 10:00 A.M. to 2:00 P.M. from May to September; call (617) 933-4929.

- Western Massachusetts Master Gardener Association hotlines. Operate from May 1 through October 1. On Monday and Thursday from 9:00 A.M. to noon, call (413) 298-5355; on Tuesday from 9:00 A.M. to noon, call (413) 533-0414.

- Barnstable County Master Gardener hotline. Open to Barnstable County residents only: (508) 375-6700. May through September: Monday to Friday 9:00 A.M. to 3:00 P.M. In April and October: Monday, Wednesday, and Friday 9:00 A.M. to 3:00 P.M. In March and November: Tuesday and Thursday 9:00 A.M. to 3:00 P.M.

3. Learn about the life and habits of the pest. The idea is to apply treatment or change your cultivation approach at the right time. (Remember the disease triangle.) Insects, for example, are most damaging at certain stages of their lives. The larval stage of Japanese beetles, the grub, devours turfgrass roots; the mature beetle eats certain flowers and leaves. Know when an insect is active so you can apply treatment when the pest is active, not dormant.

4. Examine the environment. Does the plant like where it is growing? Have you given it the conditions it needs, including the correct soil, correct sun exposure, proper moisture, enough growing space, good air circulation? Is the area around the sick plant clean, or is there debris that could harbor pests? Break the disease triangle by giving plants good soil and planting them in the right conditions.

5. Decide how much damage is too much. How much pest damage can you live with—and how much can the plant handle? Can you live with cosmetic imperfections? If so, you can tolerate a certain amount of pest damage without risking the health of the plant. You can hand pick the occasional yellowing leaf or plant a mildew-prone plant at the back of the border. But if the plant is a prominent specimen in your garden, you'll want it to look good. Scale on my favorite cherry tree by the front door made the tree look awful, so I called in a tree professional for treatment. I couldn't live with it. If the pest is threatening the life of the plant, and you want to keep the plant, you'll need to move to the next step.

6. Choose tactics to control the problem. Start with the most environmentally friendly tactic. You have lots of options other than chemicals. Tactics include cultural (better garden sanitation, crop rotation, pest-resistant varieties), physical and mechanical (floating row covers, traps, hand-picking insects), and biological (predators and natural enemies of pests). We'll talk more about tactics later. The point is, only after these tactics have failed should you consider chemical treatment (pesticides).

7. Monitor and evaluate the results. Check your garden frequently. Is your pest-control approach working, or do you need to try another tactic? Address new problems as soon as possible so you can treat them with the least toxic method.

Massachusetts Insect Pests

Of the 1.5 million known animal species on our planet, more than 1 million are insects, and fewer than 1 percent of those insects are pests. Even fewer are major pests. Problem insects in the Bay State include aphids, Asiatic beetles, dogwood borer, Eastern tent caterpillar, gypsy moth, hemlock woolly adelgid, Japanese beetles, lily leaf beetle, locust leafminer, mealybugs, white grubs, white pine weevil, and winter moth. Other common insect pests are chinch bugs, cutworms, earwigs, grubs, leafminers, mealybugs, mites, moths (and their larvae), spittlebugs, squash bugs, stink bugs, thrips, weevils, and whiteflies.

Here are IPM-oriented tactics you can apply to insect pests:

- Time your planting: Insects usually appear at about the same time every year, so plant to avoid the heaviest feeding stages. MHS master gardener Peter Coppola in Burlington modified the old baseball dictum "Hit them where they ain't" to "Grow them when they ain't." "I used to plant cool-weather crops in the spring, when the insects were active, and I had problems with the spinach and turnips," Coppola recalls. Now he plants those veggies in the fall and does not have insect damage.

- Determine when a pest is the most susceptible to a control. Control is often easiest at the egg stage, when you can remove eggs from the underside of leaves.

Bad Beetles

The beetle species in Massachusetts that go through a damaging grub stage are Japanese beetle, Asiatic garden beetle, European chafer, Oriental beetle, May beetle, and annual white grub. The Asiatic beetle is much less problematic than the Japanese beetle, while the May beetle can usually be one of the most destructive beetles here in Massachusetts.

- Protect plants from attack with physical barriers. These can include floating row covers (just make sure you don't trap overwintering larvae under the covers); collars around young plants to stop cutworms; sticky barriers; metal barriers, such as copper strips to repel slugs; and traps—rolled newspapers on the ground to catch earwigs; homemade slug traps; pheromone (hormone) bags to entice and trap flying insects.

- Attract beneficial insects—pollinators, predatory insects, and parasitoids—as well as birds and bats. (See "Encourage Beneficials," below.)

- Physically remove insects. Hand pick large beetles and caterpillars. Rub off scale. Shake asparagus beetles into a sheet. Lift spittlebugs out of their foam. Prune small branches with tent caterpillars. Spray insects off with strong spray of water if the plant is sturdy enough to handle it

- Apply an insecticide, but *only* as a last resort.

Encourage Beneficials

As gardeners we differentiate between insects that cause damage in the garden—the "bad bugs"—and those that are good for the garden because they are pollinators, predators, or parasitoids. These good bugs are called "beneficials." Predators or parasitoids are insects that attack other insects. Parasitoids are insects (such as parasitic wasps or flies) that live on or in a host insect. The adult female lays its eggs on or in the host and as the young develop they feed on the host, eventually killing it. Our beneficial garden insects include aphid midges, assassin bugs, bumblebees, common black ground beetles, dragonflies, lacewing wasps, ladybugs, praying mantis, spiders, and wasps.

Most plant-feeding insects and mites can be eaten by some other insect predator, such as a spider, mite, or daddy longleg, says Bruce Wenning, horticulturist and grounds manager for the Massachusetts Audubon Society's Habitat Wildlife Sanctuary. A ladybug, for instance, can eat more than 4,000 aphids in its life span, which is about a year. Using insect predators is not a total solution to reducing plant pests in the home landscape, he says, but predators combined with diseases can be useful biocontrols. Here's how to encourage good bugs.

1. Avoid using pesticides. Predatory insects, mites, and spiders are easily killed and repelled by insecticides and other plant-protecting chemicals.

2. Avoid planting garden plants that attract pests. Instead, plant pest-resistant species or cultivars and try to use more native plants.

3. Plant different species, not a monoculture. Diversity "provides microhabitats and food for various spiders, beetles, and other invertebrate predators," Wenning says. Beneficial insects need protection from the harsh environment that a diversified landscape provides. Use species with different bloom times, leaf and stem textures, and heights and orientations in the garden or landscape. "Leave some of your garden areas unmanaged. Use mulches and ground covers. These practices provide good hiding places for predators."

4. Add plants that attract parasitoids and predators. Plants in the pea family (Leguminosae), aster family (Compositae), mustard family (Brassicaceae), and carrot family (Umbelliferae) offer pollen and nectar for beneficial bugs.

Diseases

Plant diseases are caused by bacteria, viruses, or fungi. These pathogens are transmitted by various means: insects, the wind, rain splashing fungal spores from the ground up onto the plant, and humans. Sad to say, we gardeners inadvertently spread diseases from plant to plant by what is called poor garden sanitation: not cleaning a garden tool after using it on infected plants, touching diseased plants, touching wet plants, discarding diseased plant material improperly, or using dirty pots.

Common diseases in Massachusetts include anthracnose, bacterial wilt, cedar rust, chrysanthemum white rust, daylily rust, gray mold blight, leaf spot, potato wart, powdery mildew, and verticillium wilt.

Certain plant species are host to certain diseases. Hosts for bacterial wilt, for instance, are geraniums and solanaceous crop plants such as potatoes. "Hawthorns are easily infected by various diseases and pests, especially rusts," reports Boston-area garden coach Dr. Seija Hälvä. "If you have cedar growing nearby, that will carry cedar hawthorn rust and make the hawthorn tree look really miserable."

To minimize diseases, take steps to break the disease triangle:

- Inspect plants at the nursery to make sure they are healthy and disease free.

- Have regular soil tests done and do whatever it takes to create good soil. A good soil leads to a healthier landscape, and healthy plants are more able to shrug off diseases.

- Choose disease- or pest-resistant plants and buy certified disease-free seed. When starting plants from seed, MHS master gardener Brian Duncan in Methuen uses a HEPA filter in his basement to ensure clean air.

- Choose the right plant for your conditions; give the plant what it needs.

- When planting trees, avoid deep planting because fungal disease in the soil can more easily enter the plant through the submerged trunk.

- Water correctly, optimally at the base of a plant (see chapter 3). Water in the early part of the day so the leaves have time to dry before cooler evening temperatures.

- Avoid touching wet plants, when possible. Wash your hands or tools after touching a diseased plant. Clean tools regularly, and *always* after using them on a diseased plant.

- Rotate your crops (see chapter 6).

- Don't overcrowd your garden. Allow for good air circulation to prevent dampness and fungus.

- Keep the garden tidy to eliminate habitat for pests and disease.

- Remove the infected part of a plant or the entire plant. Dispose of diseased plants appropriately—you can bag them and leave them in the sun to cook, but since you can never be entirely sure that the pathogens have been destroyed, I would just as soon take this kind of garden debris to the dump. Do not compost diseased plant material.

Weeds

Weeds compete for everything in the garden—space, nutrients, moisture, sunlight, air. There are annual weeds, perennial weeds, grassy weeds, broadleaf weeds, woody and vining weeds. . . . Common weeds in the Bay State include chickweed, crabgrass, giant hogweed, mile-a-minute, oxeye daisy, pigweed, plantain, purslane, quack grass, tansy ragwort, and wild oat. Know what weed you are dealing with, because different weeds respond to different controls. A useful book is *Weeds of the Northeast* (see chapter 12). Hand pulling may be fine for a summer annual like pigweed (*Amaranthus*) but may never get rid of perennial Japanese knotweed (*Polygonum cuspidatum*).

The Massachusetts Department of Food and Agriculture recommends the following methods for eradicating common weeds. Its Web site (www.mass.gov) has other good information about controlling weeds. Another resource is the UMass Extension (www.umassextension.org).

Grassy summer annuals: Hand pull them, trying to remove all of the root. Do not aerate the lawn or garden when crabgrass is germinating, as it will bring weed seeds to the surface.

- Crabgrass
- Goosegrass
- Foxtails
- Barnyard grass

Broadleaved summer annuals: Mow high to shade out germinating and emerging weeds.

- Pineapple weed
- Yellow woodsorrell
- Prostrate spurge

Grassy winter annuals: Mow flower heads to prevent seed production. Correct compacted soil.

- Annual bluegrass

Broadleaved winter annuals: Hand pull, making sure you get all the roots. Mow to prevent flower heads from forming.

- Chickweed
- Shepherd's purse
- Yellow rocket

Grassy perennials: Remove clumps, including the entire root system. Aim to control during the first year of growth.

- Yellow nutsedge
- Quackgrass
- Nimbleweed
- Bromegrass

Broadleaved perennials: Mow high so the turf can outcompete the weeds. Mow the flower heads to prevent seed production.

- Dandelions
- Plantain
- Ground ivy
- Cinquefoil

You can reduce the amount of weeds that get started in your garden by cultivating less vigorously. Deep cultivation brings weed seeds to the surface. Cultivate in a way that aerates the soil, loosens it but does not turn it over too much, such as by driving in a fork and wiggling it. Mulching also reduces weed growth.

Keep weeds down—they compete with your landscape plants for everything. But you've heard the saying "A weed is just a plant in the wrong place." Some "weeds," like long meadow grasses, do provide a home for wildlife, and weeds like clover and daisies provide a food source for beneficials. There are a variety of ways to eliminate weeds: hand pulling and digging, burning with a flamer, planting so closely that weeds are shaded out. As a last resort (and often used just for invasive plants) are herbicides.

Big Pests

Deer, rabbits, voles, moles, and other furry creatures are common garden pests. Their damage is usually easy to identify. Moles tunnel to eat grubs in the soil; voles eat plants from the roots up. Rabbits leave a sharp-edged 45-degree cut when they nibble off vegetation. You'll see narrow teeth marks where rodents like mice have eaten. Deer feed on new, succulent growth and rub antlers against trees. In winter they eat evergreens and strip bark.

Some furry-pest controls include:

• Protect plants from attack with physical barriers. These can include electric fences, sonic devices to deter moles, rabbit fencing, and deer netting 8 feet tall or higher.

• Apply contact repellents or area repellents to make plants less palatable.

• Select plants that are unattractive to deer—although as far as I can tell, hungry deer will find anything attractive. In Ipswich Sally Williams, editor of the *Garden Literature Index*, maintains that the deer eat her monkshood even though it is poisonous and considered deer resistant. Arborvitae is a favorite deer snack in winter. The University of Rhode Island is testing an arborvitae replacement that seems to be deer resistant: the California incense cedar (*Calocedrus decurrens*). "It's a beautiful conifer that is rare but grows really well in our area (Zone 6)," says Dr. Brian Maynard, chair of the Department of Plant Sciences.

Pesticides, Insecticides, Herbicides

Under the IPM approach, apply pesticides or herbicides as the last resort. If you must reach for a toxic spray, try a natural or botanical product first. Use all chemical treatments carefully, even those labeled organic. Although botanical controls are derived from naturally occurring sources, *even they are not always safe for other plants, animals, and beneficial insects.* You could just as easily hurt or kill good bugs in the garden as bad bugs.

Diatomaceous earth is crushed fossilized skeletons of marine creatures. The razor-sharp particles pierce soft-bodied creatures like slugs, beetles, aphids, and spider mites so that they dehydrate. Diatomaceous earth is effective only when dry.

Horticultural oil is made from petroleum. It suffocates insects.

Insecticidal soap is made from potassium salts of fatty acids. It induces dehydration.

Milky disease (*Bacillus popillae*), sold commercially as Milky Spore, is made of bacteria that attack some but not all grubs. Once applied to the soil, it remains in the soil, continuing to infect grubs for many years.

Bt (*Bacillus thuringiensus*) is used to control caterpillars and beetles. Bt is an insecticidal baterium. It causes the breakdown of cells in the insect's gut.

Beneficial nematodes are microscopic worms that attack certain insects; different nematodes treat different insects.

Neem, a botanical derived from the neem tree, interrupts an insect's hormonal activity.

Pyrethrin compounds derived from chrysanthemums are among the most common ingredients in organic pesticides these days. To be effective these compounds must come into direct contact with the pest within about one hour of application.

Rotenone is a botanical poison made from the root of a tropical plant that can be toxic to fish and aquatic organisms. You need a permit from the state to use it near water or wetlands.

No matter what pesticide you use, natural or synthetic, *always read and follow the label.* Be certain that what you are applying matches the biology of the pest you are trying to control.

An IPM Story

Horticulturist and landscape designer Kathryn Haigh takes an IPM approach at her business, Seaside Gardens on Nantucket. "The most common pest problems here are mites (boxwoods), scale (hollies, apples), aphids (roses, annuals, and tender perennial tips), caterpillars (beach plum), moles (poor-soil lawns, bulbs), rabbits (most plants), and deer," she says.

"Planting plants where they want to grow, keeping them healthy with organic fertilizers that break down slowly in the soil, and mulching for water retention during the summer heat—these help prevent pest and fungus outbreaks a great deal," Haigh says. So does using pest- and disease-resistant cultivars. They may be more difficult to locate, but it's "worth the research."

To keep on top of things, "I perform a regimen of spraying horticultural oil in the winter before any tender buds are showing," Haigh reports. "After my early-spring pruning, I spray the branches (and the soil below persistently diseased plants) of evergreens, roses, shrubs, and trees as well as the hardscaping, like fences and sidewall shingles, where eggs or larvae may have overwintered. This is the best time to control outbreaks, as you can see the whole plant before the leaves bud out." Hardscape structures are often overlooked as hosts to pests, she notes, "but I find a lot of tiny eggs on the bottom of shingles. Later in the spring, I look for aphids on the new tips of roses and dahlias and reapply my 'hort oil.'"

It's a mistake to fertilize plants that have disease or insect infestations. You may think that a quick boost of plant food will help the plant, but all that does is create a flush of tender growth that the pest attacks with gusto. Instead, add compost to boost the soil and plant health. "Adding compost to the soil *below* problem plants rather than fertilizing them usually works and prevents the pests from attacking forced new growth from overfertilization," Haigh explains.

She is hesitant to use insecticidal soap, as it has to be reapplied often. "For beetles and cutflies on edibles, like basil and vegetables, I use a concoction of hot pepper wax and Wiltpruf, an antitranspirant."

Cultural practices, such as pinching bad leaves and providing good air circulation around susceptible plants, are your best bet for preventing fungal diseases, Haigh says. When those steps fail, however, "Wiltpruf works wonders for fungal diseases when mixed with sulfur and applied to phlox, roses, zinnias, and lilacs. The antitranspirant keeps the sulfur from washing off and coats the foliage in a clear film that blocks new spores from the leaves. I would not recommend this mix for edibles, though," she warns.

And how does she dissuade furry creatures from eating her stock? "I use a product called Deersolution to repel deer and rabbits from my perennials and roses. Its main ingredient is cinnamon oil."

Like Haigh, you can reduce pest and disease damage by practicing integrated pest management. Keep your own garden free of these "enemies," and plant intelligent, sustainable landscapes. You *will* help the big picture.

Special Challenges: City and Seaside Gardens

To round out *The Massachusetts Gardener's Companion*, I talk now about two of my favorite "flavors" of gardening, each with special needs: city gardening and seaside gardening.

City Gardens

If you're living in the city—whether it's Pittsfield, Springfield, Worcester, Brookline, or Boston—you probably won't have as much gardening space as folks in suburban and rural sections of the Bay State. But this can be a blessing. Gardeners with large plots rarely sit and relax in their gardens because there's always so much work to be done. With a small garden, you can do the spring clean-up one day, shop for plants and get them in the ground the next day, and mulch the beds on the third. On day four you can put up your feet and sip a glass of wine.

Possibly the most challenging element of urban gardening is the soil. The Western Massachusetts Master Gardener Association advises people in larger urban areas to get a soil test for possible lead contamination and other pollutants, states master gardener Nancy Howell. A soil test is essential if you plan to grow food crops. Urban soil is often exhausted, too—devoid of nutrients—and laden with castoff debris. (Turn to chapter 1 for a refresher on improving soil.)

Urban gardens provide a broader array of microclimates, enabling you to grow plants with a warmer zone rating than your friends in the suburbs can grow. Buildings and streets hold in the heat and can deflect or redirect wind. You may have a patio that captures the sun between two walls. Crisse MacFadyen in Pittsfield grows tropicals in a strip of garden squeezed between her house and her neighbor's. On the flip side, the extra heat—or the channeled wind between buildings—may cause plants to dry out rapidly.

Designing a City Garden

Just as you would with a larger garden, get to know your site: the pattern of sun and shade through the day and the growing conditions. Determine how you want to use your garden—for entertaining, relaxing, playing, or exercising? What are your privacy concerns? Do you want your garden completely screened from the street, or are you willing to give pedestrians a peek at your handiwork?

Because they are compact, urban gardens are sometimes easier to envision. You may be able to design your garden entirely from a second-floor bedroom window, as did architect Monica Sidor in Brookline. "I could see the whole garden in one fell swoop," she reports. "It was easy to get the big picture." The big picture for Sidor meant constructing her garden on top of her street-level garage, a concession to the placement of her house on a steep hill. The end result is an elegant bluestone patio, and nobody would know that her car is underfoot.

Think of your small space as a frame within which you paint

with plants. Your canvas may be small, but your palette doesn't have to be. You can make bold choices. Look at what you have: an interesting wall between you and your neighbor, lovely old trees next door, an antique fire escape, a rustic fence or hedge, or a great set of front steps that lead directly onto the street. Incorporate these hardscape elements into your design.

The hardscape becomes equal to the plants in a city garden, says horticultural historian Lucinda Brockway. "I like to use a lot of trellis and lattice applied to the walls of buildings," she says. "It creates interesting walls for the garden and allows a home for everything from espaliered fruit trees, magnolias, and other fun ornamentals to great vines." To create privacy in a Marblehead garden, Brockway erected a trellis and planted ivy, honeysuckle, and climbing hydrangea so the trellis became a living fence.

Container gardening is ideal for people who may have only a deck or patio. Group the containers creatively to build a garden without having to plant in a bed. Stagger the height of the containers, place them on steps, or hang them from fences, walls, porches, overhangs, screens, and trellises. In a small space, where the eye is drawn to colorful flowers or foliage, containers allow you to make changes quickly. When one plant stops blooming, you can exchange it for something else. Or you can rely on foliage colors and textures to make a statement.

Great City Plants

What plants work well in city gardens? Often your plant choices are determined by how much light your garden receives. Diane Martin had to contend with two big old trees in her Newton neighbor's yard that almost completely blocked the sun from her garden. With her neighbor's go-ahead, she pruned the trees but still found little sun getting through. Undaunted, she incorporated unusual shade plants into her design and hung plants on the walls to catch what sun there is. She took a limitation and made of it an elegant garden for evening cocktails and dinner.

Plants for Small Gardens

- Maple (*Acer ginnala* 'Emerald Elf')
- Dwarf Alberta spruce (*Picea glauca conica*)
- Weigelia (*Weigelia* 'Midnight Wine')
- Mugho pine (*Pinus mugho* 'Slow Mound')
- Daphne spirea (*Spiraea japonica* 'Alpina')
- Cypress (*Chamaecyparis* 'Nana Gracilis')
- Lilac (*Syringa* x *vulgaris* 'Prairie Petite')
- Miscanthus (*Miscanthus* 'Kleine Fontaine')
- Moor grass (*Sesleria nitida*)
- Wormwood (*Artemesia* 'Silver Mound')
- Bellflower (*Campanula* 'Blue Harebells')
- Coral bells (*Heuchera* 'Chocolate Ruffles')
- Daylily (*Hemerocallis* 'Stella d'Oro')
- Chrysanthemum (*Chrysanthemum* 'White Bomb')

Shrubs and small trees will grow in containers, especially if you have space in a garage or basement to overwinter them. A list of wonderful small trees and shrubs appears in the sidebar "Plants for Small Gardens." You also can keep a larger shrub small by means of judicious pruning.

Sally Williams, editor of the *Garden Literature Index,* has developed the following list of trouble-free, high-performing perennials. She grows these in her Boston garden. All but the speedwell are native plants.

False indigo (*Baptisia australis*). "The blue green foliage glows all summer, the dark seedpods are interesting, and after frost the blackened foliage is a startling contrast," Williams says. False indigo is well behaved, gradually forming a large clump, and is pest-free, she adds.

Speedwell (*Veronica spicata*). This blue flower will rebloom if cut back and is a good foil for daylilies, she says.

Coneflower (*Echinacea purpurea*). "Woodchucks 'prune' it in spring, which delays bloom," Williams admits. "But I keep it because it then flowers late when blooms are scarce."

Sneezeweed (*Helenium autumnale* 'Moorheim Beauty'). She describes this as a glorious, dark red, long bloomer.

Blue star (*Amsonia hubrichtii*). "Lovely willowy foliage turns golden in autumn."

Aster (*Aster divaricatus* or *Eurybia divaricata*). This native wood aster delights with small but numerous white flowers.

Goldenrod (*Solidago ohioensis*). "Wide flower heads are an uncommon sulphury lemony yellow," Williams says.

Phlox (*Phlox stolonifera*). "A wonderful ground cover for sun or shade," she states. "Pale blue spring flowers shimmer like waves of water."

Twinleaf (*Jeffersonia diphylla*). Its elegant white spring flower is unfortunately ephemeral, Williams notes, but it retains lovely, long-lasting foliage.

City gardeners don't have to go without home-grown produce. Tomatoes, peppers, beans, and strawberries thrive beautifully in pots. Different lettuce varieties make a gorgeous display when grouped together. Don't be afraid to interplant vegetables with nonedible flowering plants.

Garden coach Dr. Seija Hälvä in Cambridge created her garden from a paved yard that was formerly used as a parking lot. She cleared the paving and amended the soil, and now she harvests peaches, plums, apricots, currants, gooseberries, and many other edibles from that backyard. "This kind of gardening requires lots of work, but the reward is tasty and satisfying," Hälvä says. "The growing season is clearly warmer and longer in the city, which is great for many vegetables and fruit."

Encouraging Wildlife

Low-maintenance options for city gardens include mossy Japanese gardens, says Hälvä. These could include a soothing water feature to provide "a calming contrast to the ever-humming city." Water features are also useful for attracting wildlife to your urban garden.

Wildlife has a place even in a city. Birds and butterflies bring life and whimsy to a garden. Bruce Wenning, grounds manager of the Massachusetts Audubon Society's Habitat Education Center and Wildlife Sanctuary in Belmont, offers these suggestions for attracting birds and wildlife to your garden.

- Plant vegetation of different species, growth habits (height, color, plant form), and bloom times.

- Include several nut-bearing or fruit-bearing trees and shrubs to attract birds. Birds particularly like dark berries, Wenning says.

- Allow space for tall herbaceous plants, including grasses and even weeds! These provide nectar for beneficial insects and hiding places for ground-dwelling creatures.

- Add a water source, such as a birdbath.

- Plant shrubs and evergreens and include rock walls or rock groups. These give birds and other wildlife protection from predators and harsh winter winds.

And of course you can attract birds and other wildlife by putting out birdseed, suet, and other appropriate foods.

A city garden can accomplish a lot in a compact space. One garden accessory will give a pocket garden drama, whereas single accents get lost in a huge landscape. Incorporate views into your garden for passers-by and you improve the aesthetic of your neighborhood. Nothing beats strolling around a city and gazing over garden gates and down garden paths. Whenever I peek into the sunken gardens in Nantucket or the dooryard gardens in Marblehead, I'm in heaven.

Seaside Gardening

Talk to people who garden by the sea and you'll find they all face similar challenges—salt and wind. "Northeast or northwest winter winds desiccate plants and carry damaging salt sprays, making it a struggle for even the hardiest plants to thrive," explains Barbara Dombrowski of Goose Cove Gardens in Gloucester. John Bartlett of Bartlett's Farm on Nantucket agrees: "We often get 50 mile-per-hour winds here, and it can be really difficult to grow under those conditions. We also can have very cool springs; the ocean keeps us warm in the fall but cool in the spring."

The open, windswept seaside landscape offers bountiful sun, but too much sun can be as much a problem as an asset, adds David Bartsch of David Bartsch Landscape Architects on Nantucket.

Designing a Seaside Garden

How can seaside gardeners cope with their intrinsic challenges? Using raised beds and containers gives you a little more control over soil and water conditions, says Katie Haried of Katie Haried Landscape Designs in Newburyport. "They are easier on your back for planting and weeding," she adds. Adding a screen or a stone wall will create microclimates that will help some plants to survive in areas that might otherwise be a problem, Haried says.

David Bartsch tries to "glean the most opportunities possible from a property's natural setting, and then build on that existing context. At the ocean, that means creating windbreaks, maximizing views, and creating unique spaces to form a whole composition." Water features can complement a view to the ocean. "And earthworks, plantings, walls, and other structures help to define spaces, create privacy, and direct views for areas such as games courts or outdoor dining/cooking areas."

Right Plant, Right Site

"Planting for the conditions is even more important at or near the shore, as the environment can be unforgiving," asserts Haried. The water table can be high near the coast, which dumps extra

salt on the root zone and often leaves plants with wet feet. "I know these are all obvious facts," she says, "but too often we fall in love with a plant that will not thrive or even survive these conditions, and then we are disappointed when it doesn't work."

"When you're dealing with salt, wind, full sun with little rain, and difficult soil, putting the right plant in the right place will vastly improve the plant's chance of success and reduce your maintenance tasks trying to coax it to survive," agrees David Bartsch. Some of the best-performing seaside plants have gray foliage, such as santolina or artemesia. Other plants he finds that do well are plants that grow naturally in seaside conditions, like *Rosa rugosa,* viburnums, bayberry, and clethra.

Kathryn Haigh of Seaside Gardens in Nantucket agrees with Bartsch's choice of gray plants and finds that on the ocean, simple is better: "saline-tolerant plants that don't mind gale force winds and the occasional hurricane blast," she says. When it comes to roses, "old-garden roses seem to be the hardiest, whether they are shrub, climbing, or bush roses," Haigh states. "Fog makes more fussy varieties look bad in July and August when black spot and powdery mildew set in."

Abigail Austin at Goose Cove Gardens in Gloucester tells of a garden at the edge of the cove that gets flooded during winter high tides. "It is planted with German iris, 'Autumn Joy' sedum, and daylilies," she says. "None of these seem bothered at all by the sporadic salt water."

Goose Cove Gardens owner Barbara Dombrowski recommends some of her favorite perennials for salt- and windswept gardens:

- Wormwood (*Artemesia* spp.)
- Montauk daisy (*Nipponanthemum nipponicum*)
- Sea lavender (*Limonium latifolium*)
- Thyme
- Daylilies (*Hemerocallis)*
- Sea holly (*Eryngium maritimum*)
- Bearded iris
- Coreopsis
- Obedient plant (*Physostegia virginiana*)
- Sedum
- Hydrangea

These are some of my favorites:
- Panic grass (*Panicum amarum* 'Dewey Blue')
- Black fountain grass (*Pennisetum alopecuroides* 'Moudry')
- Miscanthus (*Miscanthus sinensis* 'Morning Light')
- Leatherleaf sedge (*Carex buccchanii*)
- Russian sage (*Perovskia atriplicifolia*)
- Coneflower (*Rudbeckia sullivantii* 'Goldsturm')
- Chrysanthemum (*Chrysanthemum* 'Sheffield Pink')
- Daylily (*Hemerocallis* 'Happy Returns')

- Stonecrop (*Sedum spurium* 'Dragon's Blood')
- Mugwort or sagebrush (*Artemesia stelleriana* 'Silver Brocade')
- Pine (*Pinus thumbergii* 'Thunderhead')
- Spruce (*Picea pungens glauca* 'Montgomery Blue')

Katie Haried reminds us that sticking with natives and purchasing locally grown stock "greatly enhances chances of success."

Challenges aside, Kathryn Haigh admits that she is spoiled by Nantucket's Zone 7 climate and ocean breezes. "Gardening is a little more challenging because of exposure issues and the inevitable late spring storms and frosts, but it's definitely not difficult. It is all in a gardener's plant knowledge."

CHAPTER TWELVE

Resources for the Massachusetts Gardener

This chapter gives you a sampling of gardening resources in the state. But perhaps some of the best resources are your neighborhood garden centers and your local garden clubs. There are a lot of good gardeners in Massachusetts—talk to them! You can also learn from horticultural societies, master gardener associations, garden clubs, workshops, flower shows, lectures, plant sales, and organized garden tours.

University of Massachusetts Extension

The UMass Extension is headquartered at 101 University Drive on the Amherst campus; (413) 545–4800; www.umassextension.org. Local cooperative extension offices are in Barnstable, Boston, Brockton, East Wareham, Fall River, Hanson, Lawrence, Pittsfield, South Hadley, Springfield, Walpole, Waltham, and Worcester. You can find their contact information at www.umassextension .org/about/locations.html.

Although there is no hotline for home owners, the UMass Extension offers a gold mine of information through its Web sites. You'll find specific plant information, all sorts of fact sheets and print materials, and details about events such as the UMass Small Farm and Garden Days. The Web sites include:

- Landscape, Nursery & Urban Forestry: www.umassgreen info.org (the site most commonly visited by home owners)
- Agriculture & Landscape Program: www.umass.edu/agland
- Center for Agriculture: www.masscenterforag.org
- Cranberries: www.umass.edu/cranberries/
- Fruit: www.umass.edu/fruitadvisor/
- Integrated Pest Management: www.umass.edu/umext/ipm/
- Soil Testing: www.umass.edu/soiltest
- Turf: www.umassturf.org
- Vegetables: www.umassvegetable.org

Master Gardener Hotlines

The following hotlines are staffed by certified master gardeners, trained volunteers who help the public with gardening questions. Master gardeners have been through a forty-hour training course and have put in an equal number of hours in volunteer time to the community, then they keep their skills polished through additional training and volunteer work each year. For help with your gardening problems, or to find out more about becoming a master gardener, call the hotlines or visit the Web sites.

Massachusetts Horticultural Society Master Gardener Program (www.masshort.org). The MHS HortLine operates Monday, Wednesday, and Friday 10:00 A.M. to 2:00 P.M. year-round; Saturday 10:00 A.M. to 2:00 P.M. from May to September; call (617) 933–4929. Plant clinics are held periodically throughout the year.

Western Massachusetts Master Gardener Association (www.wmassmastergardeners.org). Hotlines operate from May 1 through October 1. On Monday and Thursday from 9:00 A.M. to noon, call (413) 298–5355; on Tuesday from 9:00 A.M. to noon, call (413) 533–0414. Voice mail operates year-round.

Barnstable County Master Gardener Program. Hotline is open to Barnstable County residents only: (508) 375–6700. Hours from May through September: Monday to Friday 9:00 A.M. to 3:00 P.M. In April and October: Monday, Wednesday, and Friday 9:00 A.M. to 3:00 P.M. In March and November: Tuesday and Thursday 9:00 A.M. to 3:00 P.M. Closed December through February.

Garden Clubs and Organizations

Massachusetts Horticultural Society (www.masshort.org). Founded in 1829, the Massachusetts Horticultural Society is a venerable horticultural and educational institution offering many courses plus a library and education center. It presents the New England Spring Flower Show in Boston each March.

Worcester Horticultural Society (www.towerhillbg.org). Headquartered at Tower Hill, the Worcester County Horticultural Society is the third oldest horticultural society in the country. It holds flower shows throughout the year.

New England Wild Flower Society (www.newfs.org). One of the most active and substantial plant societies in the country, the New England Wild Flower Society focuses on native plantings and wildflowers and educates about conservation and eradicating invasive plants.

American Horticultural Society (www.ahs.org). A highly respected horticultural organization, the AHS (founded in 1922) is one of the oldest national garden organizations in the country.

Garden Club Federation of Massachusetts (www.gcfm.org). With almost 200 member garden clubs in Massachusetts, this organization produces spectacular flower shows, and local clubs serve their communities through volunteer beautification projects.

Massachusetts Nursery and Landscape Association (www.mnla.com). MNLA's *Hometown Guide* lists member landscape contractors and nurseries by town; its *A Pocket Guide to Native and Low Maintenance Woody Plants for the Massachusetts Landscape* is one of the best on the subject.

Public Gardens

Arnold Arboretum of Harvard University, 125 Arborway, Jamaica Plain 02138; (617) 524–1718; www.arboretum.harvard.edu. This 265-acre arboretum is the oldest in the country, with trees and shrubs from around the world.

Berkshire Botanical Garden, 5 West Stockbridge Road, Routes 102 and 183, Stockbridge 01262; (413) 298–3926; www.berk shirebotanical.org. One of the oldest public display gardens in the country, the fifteen-acre garden features an herb garden, a perennial garden, a shade garden, the Rice Greenhouse, an exhibit hall, and a host of educational programs.

Case Estates, 135 Wellesley Street, Weston 02493; (617) 524–1718. A sixty-five-acre reservation with lovely gardens, rare plant specimens including evergreens, and a fine rhododendron display garden maintained by the Massachusetts Chapter of the American Rhododendron Society.

Durfee Conservatory, University of Massachusetts, 230 Stockbridge Road, Amherst 01003; (413) 545–5234; www .umass.edu/durfee. An underpublicized arboretum and conservatory established in 1867 on the campus at UMass Amherst. The glasshouses contain a rain-forest room, Victorian collection, bamboo meditation garden, orchids, and more.

Elm Bank Reservation, Route 16, Wellesley 02482; (617) 933–4900; www.masshort.org. The thirty-six-acre home of the Massachusetts Horticultural Society's horticulture and education center and the All-America Selections trial gardens. Elm Bank is a hub of horticultural activity and information, from classes and lectures to gardens and greenhouses, a plant clinic, and events.

Garden in the Woods, 180 Hemenway Road, Framingham 01701; (508) 877–7630; www.newfs.org. Headquarters of the New England Wild Flower Society, this ever-changing living museum showcases more than 1,600 kinds of plants, many of them rare and endangered native specimens. It holds a spectacular annual plant sale and offers classes.

Heritage Plantation Gardens, 130 Grove Street, Sandwich 02537; (508) 888–3300; www.heritageplantation.org. This seventy-six-acre garden is a showplace of thousands of colorful, distinctive rhododendrons.

Mount Holyoke College Botanic Garden, 50 College Street, South Hadley 01075; (413) 538–2116; www.myholyoke.edu/offices/botan/. This garden consists of three main parts: the campus gardens of herbaceous perennials, trees, and shrubs; the campus arboretum, with a collection of woody trees and shrubs; and the Talcott Greenhouse, a Victorian-era complex featuring nonhardy plants from around the world.

Nasami Farm, 128 North Street, Whatley, 01373; (413) 397–9922; www.newfs.org. The seventy-five-acre garden is the New England Wild Flower Society's native plant nursery and education center. Its 375 native plant species include perennials, trees, shrubs, vines, and ferns.

Polly Hill Arboretum, 809 State Road, West Tisbury 02575; (508) 693–9426; www.pollyhillarboretum.org. This seventy-acre horticultural landmark on Martha's Vineyard was first planted as an arboretum in 1958 by Polly Hill herself.

Smith College Botanical Gardens and Lyman Conservatory, Smith College, Northampton 01060; (413) 585–2740; www.smith.edu/garden. A campus arboretum, numerous plant collections, 12,000 square feet of glasshouses, and more than 10,000 kinds of plants.

Stanley Park, 400 Western Avenue, Westfield 01086; (413) 568–9312; www.stanleypark.org. Winner of the AARS Outstanding Public Rose Garden Award, these wonderful gardens include fifty varieties of roses and 2,500 rosebushes.

Tower Hill Botanic Garden, 11 French Drive, Boylston 01505; (508) 869–6111; www.towerhillbg.org. Tower Hill, with 132 acres of gardens, meadows, woodlands, trails, and a seasonal display of 95,000 flowering bulbs, is the home of the Worcester County Horticultural Society.

Additionally, each July/August issue of *People, Places & Plants* (www.ppplants.com) lists all of the public gardens in New England, including some sixty in Massachusetts.

Books

Building a Healthy Lawn by Stuart Franklin

Carrots Love Tomatoes by Louis Riotte

Coastal Plants from Cape Cod to Cape Canaveral by Irene H. Stuckey & Lisa Lofland Gould

The Complete Gardener's Almanac: A Month by Month Guide to Successful Gardening by Marjorie Willison

Drought-Tolerant Plants: Waterwise Gardening for Every Climate by Jane Taylor

The Four Season Harvest by Eliot Coleman

A Gardener's Guide to Frost: Outwit the Weather and Extend the Spring and Fall Seasons by Philip Harnden

Garden Insects of North America: The Ultimate Guide to Backyard Bugs by Whitney Cranshaw

The Garden Primer by Barbara Damrosch

Gardens of the New Republic: Fashioning the Landscapes of High Street, Newburyport, Massachusetts by Lucinda A. Brockway and Lindsay H. Cavanagh

Handbook of Successful Organic Lawn Care by Paul D. Sachs

Insect and Mite Pests of Shade Trees and Woody Ornamentals by Robert Childs and Jennifer Konieczny

Just the Facts! by Garden Way Publishing

The Lawn Bible by David Mellor

Meetings with Remarkable Trees by Thomas Pakenham

National Audubon Society's Field Guide to New England

Native Trees, Shrubs and Vines by William Cullina

The Natural Shade Garden by Ken Druse

The New England Gardener's Book of Lists by Karan Davis Cutler

The New York Times 1,000 Gardening Questions & Answers

A Northeast Gardener's Year by Lee Reich

The Organic Gardener's Home Reference: A Plant-by-Plant Guide to Growing Fresh, Healthy Food by Tanya Denckla

The Organic Lawn Care Manual by Paul Tukey

Park's Success with Seeds by Anne Reilly

The Perennial Gardener by Frederick McGourty

A Pocket Guide to Native and Low Maintenance Woody Plants for the Massachusetts Landscape by the Massachusetts Nursery and Landscape Association

The Practical Gardener by Roger Swain

The Private Life of Plants by David Attenborough

Rodale's Illustrated Encyclopedia of Organic Gardening, Pauline Pears, editor

The Rose by the American Rose Society

Roses Love Garlic by Louis Riotte

Roses: A Care Manual by Amanda Beales

Seascape Gardening: from New England to the Carolinas by Anne Halpin and Roger Foley

The Vegetable Gardener's Bible by Edward C. Smith

Weeds of the Northeast by Richard H. Uva, Joseph C. Neal, and Joseph M. DiTomaso

Media

Fine Gardening (www.FineGardening.com). An excellent magazine with a section specific to New England. They also publish a selection of books.

Garden Guys **radio show** (www.garden-guys.com). "Talk Radio Goes Organic"—Sam Jeffries and Fred Jackson, the Garden Guys, answer on-air garden questions Sunday from 8:00 to 10:00 A.M. on WHJJ 920AM; call (866) 920–9455. Great radio show best heard in southern Massachusetts, but it will soon be broadcasting to a greater range and larger audience. Each week they have guests and take your questions on air.

Horticulture (www.hortmag.com). A venerable horticultural institution; the magazine has a regional section for New England. Also publishes garden books.

People, Places & Plants (www.ppplants.com). A magazine that focuses exclusively on gardening in the Northeast. Also produces a television show of the same name on HGTV hosted by Roger Swain and Paul Tukey.

Annuals and Perennials

All-America Rose Selections (www.rose.org). A nonprofit association of rose growers and introducers dedicated to the introduction and promotion of exceptional roses.

All-America Selections (www.all-americaselections.org). A non-profit organization that evaluates plants impartially.

American Rose Society (www.ars.org). A wealth of information about roses.

Blooms of Bressingham (www.bloomsofbressingham.com). Branded plants.

New England Rose Society (www.rosepetals.org). Based in Worcester.

Perennial Plant Association (www.perennialplant.org). A professional trade association that selects and promotes one perennial plant each year.

Perry's Perennial Plants (www.uvm.edu/~pass/perry/). Dr. Leonard Perry, extension professor at the University of Vermont, shares his expertise on this Web site.

Proven Winners (www.provenwinners.com). Branded plants.

USDA Plant Database (www.plants.usda.gov). A national database of plant information. You can see a listing of plants in your state, wetlands in the state, endangered plants all over the United States, and noxious and invasive plants, and you can contribute plant information.

Climate, Weather, and Water

Clean Air—Cool Planet and **University of New Hampshire Climate Education Initiative** (www.cleanair-coolplanet.org; www.sustainableunh.unh.edu/climate_ed). Partnered Web sites give data on global warming and show ways you can help stop or slow the trend.

Groundwater Foundation (www.groundwater.org).

Massachusetts State Government (www.mass.gov/agr/water wellbeing_facts.htm). The state government's helpful Web site with information about water, water use, and lawn care.

National Atlas of the United States of America (www.national atlas.gov). Look under Climate to locate a map of Massachusetts with the precipitation clearly illustrated.

National Drought Mitigation Center (http://drought.unl.edu/ dm/monitor). A drought-monitoring site.

National Ground Water Association (www.ngwa.org).

National Weather Service (www.nws.noaa.gov).

Rain Barrel Guide (www.rainbarrelguide.com). An excellent guide to rain barrels, with names of suppliers.

U.S. Geological Survey (www.usgs.gov). Compiles water use estimates for counties in the United States; find details under Drought Watch.

USDA Hardiness Zone Map (www.usna.usda.gov/Hardzone/ ushzmap.html). View hardiness zones for any part of the United States.

Water Systems Council (www.watersystemscouncil.org).

Wunderground (www.wunderground.com). A fun site with lots of climate data.

Invasive Plants

Center for Invasive Plant Management (www.weedcenter.org). A good overview of the national problem, but less focused on the Northeast.

Ecology and Management of Invasive Plants Program (www.invasiveplants.net). Focuses on work conducted by students and staff at Cornell University.

Greater Worcester Land Trust (www.gwlt.org).

Invasive Plant Atlas of New England (www.invasives.uconn .edu). Detailed lists of all the invasive plant species.

Massachusetts Aquatic Invasive Species Working Group (www.state.ma.us/czm/invasivemanagementplan.htm). A coalition of Massachusetts state agencies, federal government officials, consultants, and others to recognize the potentially devastating impacts of non-native species on marine and freshwater environments.

Massachusetts Introduced Pests Outreach Project (www.mass nrc.org). A wealth of information and fact sheets about pests, diseases, and invasives.

Massachusetts Invasive Plant Advisory Group (www.massnrc .org/MIPAG). A collaborative of Massachusetts organizations, state and federal agencies, and professionals concerned with the conservation of the Massachusetts natural landscape.

Massachusetts Prohibited Plant List (www.mass.gov/agr/farm products/proposed_prohibited_plant_list_v12-12-05.htm). The official list of 141 species.

National Gardening Association (www.garden.org/weedlibrary). Comprehensive list of weeds.

National Invasive Species Information Center (www.invasive specisinfo.gov).

Natural Heritage & Endangered Species Program, Massachusetts Division of Fisheries and Wildlife (www.nhesp.org).

Nature Conservancy (www.nature.org).

New England Wild Flower Society (www.newfs.org). A mecca for any gardener interested in native plants and for those seeking solutions to the problem of invasive plants. The Web site includes the Massachusetts Prohibited Plant List and a list of native substitutes for ornamental invasives.

Rhode Island Natural History Survey (www.rinhs.org).

United States National Arboretum (www.usna.usda.gov/gardens/ invasives.html).

Wild Ones (www.for-wild.org). A nonprofit national educational organization seeking to educate its members and the community about the benefits of using local native plant species in natural landscaping. It does not currently have a chapter in Massachusetts but would like to start one.

Land and Turf Care

Living Lawn Project (www.livinglawn.org). The site offers the downloadable brochure *Simple Steps Towards a Healthy Lawn;* the project's demonstration garden is in Marblehead.

Massachusetts Department of Agricultural Resources (www.mass.gov/agr/gardening/turf/index.htm). Download *A Homeowner's Guide to Environmentally Sound Lawn Care.*

Northeast Organic Farming Association (www.nofa.org, www.nofamass.org). A tremendous source of organic information for the home gardener and small farmer. Publications include *A Citizen's Guide to Organic Land Care,* the *Organic Food Guide* and the *NOFA Guide to Organic Land Care: the Directory of Accredited Organic Land Care Professionals in the Northeast.* A handbook on organic lawn and turf care is forthcoming.

Safe Lawns (www.safelawns.org). A collaborative effort of garden professionals to educate gardeners and home owners about nontoxic lawn care.

Skogley Memorial Turfgrass Research Facility, University of Rhode Island (www.uri.edu/cels/pls/outreachturf.html). Read about the research at one of the oldest turfgrass research centers in the country.

Toxics Information Project (www.toxicsinfo.org). Publishes the *Less Toxic Landscaping Resource Directory* that lists land care professionals who use nontoxic methods and products.

Toxics Use Reduction Institute (www.turi.org). A Massachusetts state-funded institute and part of a program based on the

Toxics Use Reduction Act of 1989. Download its *10 Tips for a Healthy, Pesticide-free Lawn.*

Turf Resource Center (www.TurfGrassSod.org). Nonprofit, online source of detailed and general information for both the consumer and the industry.

Landscape Architects or Designers

American Society of Landscape Architects (www.asla.org). Click on Products & Services and type in "Massachusetts" to get a listing of all member landscape architects.

Association of Professional Landscape Designers (www.apld .com; New England region: www.apldne.org). Offers a certification program to encourage professional recognition and standards. Visit the New England site and click on Find a Designer.

Conway School of Landscape Design (www.csld.edu). Provides referrals of alumni within a localized search area. You can request the services of a student designer if you live within thirty minutes of the school. Visit online and click on Alumni Links, or call the office at (413) 369–4044.

Pests and Diseases

Refer also to the "Master Gardener Hotlines" section at the beginning of this chapter.

The Landscape Message (www.umassgreeninfo.org). A compilation of information gathered by UMass Extension scouts monitoring landscape sites statewide for local pest activity.

Massachusetts Integrated Pest Management Council (www.mass .gov/agr/ipmcouncil/index.htm). Promotes IPM practices and education within urban and other settings.

Massachusetts Introduced Pests Outreach Project (www.mass nrc.org/pests/factsheets.htm). A collaboration between the UMass Extension Agriculture and Landscape Program and the Massachusetts Department of Agricultural Resources. Fact sheets on a huge number of insects, weeds, diseases, and nematodes; links for reporting pest sightings; and other resources.

Northeastern IPM Center (www.NortheastIPM.org). Part of a nationwide system established by the USDA to provide information about integrated pest management across the Northeast.

Soil

Bureau of Waste Prevention, Massachusetts Department of Environmental Protection (www.mass.gov/dep/recycle). Find a town compost site in your area.

Composters.com (www.composters.com). An online source of worm bins and "worm accessories"; find additional composting Web sites by typing "purchasing worm bins" into an online search engine.

Office of the State Soil Scientist (www.soils.usda.gov). Excellent USDA Web site with in-depth information on soils and weather. Research the soil surveys for your county's soil from this site. Or write to the local office: Office of the State Soil Scientist, USDA Natural Resources Conservation Service, 451 West Street, Amherst 01002.

Soil Science Society of America (www.soils.org). Lists good publications about soils and crops.

Soil Tests

University of Massachusetts Extension Service (www.umass.edu/ plsoils/soiltest). UMass Amherst offers a variety of soil and compost tests for a relatively small fee. Get details online or write to the Soil and Plant Tissue Testing Laboratory, West Experiment Station, 682 North Pleasant Street, University of Massachusetts, Amherst 01003. UMass Amherst soil sample kits are often sold in local garden centers.

Trees and Shrubs

Cary Award (www.caryaward.org). Promotes outstanding plants for New England gardens.

Massachusetts Arborists' Association (www.massarbor.org). Provides referrals and links to www.certifiedtreeandlawn.org.

National Arbor Day Foundation (www.arborday.org/treeinfo/treehealth.cfm). Offers links to certified arborists.

Tree Care Industry Association (www.tcia.org). Accredits tree care companies and establishes standards of tree care practice. Visit the Web site and enter your zip code to find a certified arborist in your area.

University of Rhode Island Cooperative Extension and Department of Plant Sciences (www.uri.edu/research/sustland). Offers an online list of sustainable trees and shrubs for New England.

Vegetables

Community Supported Agriculture (www.umassvegetable.org/food_farming_systems/CSA/farms_ma.html). Learn more about community supported agriculture and locate local farms that will sell you vegetables through this program.

Farmers' markets (www.mass.gov/agr/massgrown/farmers_markets.htm). A directory of farmers' markets and wineries around the state, a calendar of events, a complete list of Massachusetts-grown products, an agriculture tourism map, and a download-able poster, all from the Massachusetts Department of Agricultural Resources.

University of Massachusetts Extension (www.umassvegetable
.org; www.nevegetable.org). Features *The New England Vegetable
Management Guide*, a collaborative effort of members of the
extension vegetable programs of the Universities of Maine,
New Hampshire, Vermont, Connecticut, and Massachusetts.

Wildlife

Massachusetts Audubon Society (www.massaudubon.org).
Information about wildlife and encouraging wildlife in your
garden, plus a list of wildlife sanctuaries. Wildlife Information
Line: (781) 259–2150.

USDA Wildlife Services–Massachusetts; (413) 253–2403.
Damage control of problem animals.

Glossary

acid soil: Soil with a pH lower than 7.

alkaline soil: Soil with a pH higher than 7.

annual: A plant that germinates, grows to maturity, sets seed, and dies all in one growing season.

antitranspirant: A solution sprayed on plants to decrease water loss through foliage.

bacteria: Organisms that cause disease.

balled and burlapped: A tree or shrub dug from the ground with a ball of soil around the roots that has been wrapped in burlap or similar material.

bare root: A plant with no soil or very little soil around the roots.

biennial: A plant that germinates, grows to maturity, sets seed, and dies over a two-year period.

botanical controls: Products derived from naturally occurring sources that are used to eradicate weeds and other noxious plants.

branch collar: The area at the base of a branch where it meets the trunk.

caliper: A measurement of the diameter of a tree's trunk.

clay soils: Soils predominantly made of tiny mineral particles.

climate: Weather conditions that happen in a specific region.

cold frame: A box, with a see-through lid, that is set in the ground and into which plants are either sown or set in pots to protect them against the cold.

companion planting: A planting technique in which plants that are thought to protect or benefit each other are grown in the same area.

compost: A product of decomposed organic matter, usually made by a balance of "brown" and "green" plant material.

compost tea: A brew made by steeping compost in water; used as a foliar spray or liquid fertilizer.

container grown: Referring to a plant that was started and grown in a container.

cool-weather crops: Plants that do not tolerate heat and are therefore more likely to be early spring or fall crops.

corn gluten meal: A product used to eliminate weeds; it works by stopping a germinating plant's root formation.

cover crops: Plants that are grown for a season and then tilled into the soil, thus putting organic matter back into the soil. Also known as green manure.

crop rotation: A planting technique that ensures plants from the same botanical family are not grown in the same spot every year.

damping-off: A fungal disease that is often a problem during seed germination.

deadheading: Pinching or cutting spent blooms to stimulate the plant to put energy into new blooms.

diatomaceous earth: Crushed fossilized skeletons of marine creatures used to control some insects.

disease triangle: An approach to understanding how plant disease develops; states that three factors must be present: a susceptible plant, a pathogen, and the right environmental conditions.

drip irrigation: A method of watering that uses hoses with tiny outlets called emitters that dispense water directly to the soil at targeted spots.

field grown: Referring to plants that are started in the field and later dug up and grown in a container.

fungal diseases: Diseases caused by fungus; rot, decay, and mold are indicators of fungal disease.

glacial till: A mix of sand, silt, and clay that resulted from glacier action.

growing season: The number of days between the last frost of the spring and the first of the fall.

grub: Larva stage of an insect during its life cycle.

half-hardy annuals: Annual plants that can handle a slight frost.

half-hardy perennials: Plants that need some protection (such as mulch) from winter cold.

hardening off: The process of acclimatizing plants grown indoors to outdoor temperatures.

hardiness zone: Usually refers to a USDA Hardiness Zone designation, one of eleven areas, or zones, each based on a 10-degree Fahrenheit difference in average annual minimum temperatures. Plant hardiness zones are used to help identify which plants will survive low temperatures.

hardy annuals: Annuals that can be sown outdoors in spring, before the last frost, as soon as the ground can be worked. Some can be sown in the fall for spring germination.

hardy perennials: Plants that can survive very cold winters without protection or with very little protection.

herbaceous perennial: A plant with stems, leaves, and flowers that die back to the ground in fall and regrow in spring.

herbicide: A substance that kills plants.

hoop house: A hooped structure for protecting plants; can be as large as a greenhouse or small and movable.

horticultural oil: A substance that is sprayed on plants to suffocate insects.

insecticide: A substance that kills insects.

insecticidal soap: A substance made from potassium salts of fatty acids used to control or kill insects.

integrated pest management (IPM): A commonsense, ecologically friendly method of dealing with the problems of disease and pest damage, with an emphasis on using the least toxic approach.

interplanting: Growing two or more crops together in the same place to their mutual benefit.

invasive plants: Plants not native to the United States that crowd out native species and cause environmental and economic harm.

irrigation zones: An area where plants with similar water needs are grown together.

leader: A main tree stem or trunk.

leaf scar: The mark left on a branch when a leaf falls off.

lime: Calcium carbonate; used to raise the soil pH level.

loam: A balanced mix of sand, silt, and clay with good texture, good drainage, and the right amounts of moisture and air.

manure: Animal droppings often used as a soil amendment.

microbial activity: The activity of microbes in the soil.

microclimate: Pockets of warmer or colder temperatures within a hardiness zone.

milky disease: A bacteria (*Bacillus popillae*) that attacks some but not all grubs in the soil.

mulch: Compost, wood chips, buckwheat hulls, or other materials applied on top of soil to help conserve water and keep weeds down.

native plant: A plant that has been growing in North America since before European settlement.

neem: An organic insecticide derived from the neem tree; it interrupts hormonal activity.

nematodes: Microscopic worms that attack insects.

neutral soil: Soil with a pH of 7.0, which is midway between acid and alkaline.

nutrients: The elements needed by a plant for healthy growth.

organic matter: Material made by plants and animals.

parasitoid: Referring to insect parasites that live on or in a host insect.

parent material: The third soil layer, or horizon, which roots cannot penetrate.

pheromone traps: Devices filled with insect hormones and used to trap insects.

Paxton soil: The official state soil of Massachusetts, named after the town of Paxton in Worcester County.

perennial: A plant that comes back and lives year after year.

pH: A measurement of how alkaline or acid the soil. The measurements range from 1 to 14, with 1 to 5 acidic, 8 to 14 alkaline, and 6 to 7 considered neutral.

pollinator: An insect that transfers pollen from the anther to the stigma in a flower.

predators: Insects that attack other insects.

rain barrel: A container to catch rainwater, usually placed at the bottom of a downspout.

rhizomes: Stems that travel under the surface of the soil.

sandy soils: Soils predominantly made of large mineral particles.

self-sowers: Annuals or biennials that deposit their seeds in the garden and the seeds germinate the following year.

silty soils: Soils made predominantly of medium-size mineral particles.

soaker hose: An irrigation hose that "sweats" water along its entire length.

sod: Fully grown turf that is cut in strips ready to be laid in a prepared bed to create an instant lawn.

soil amendments: Materials added to the soil to improve it, such as animal manure, slow-release organic fertilizers, cover crops, and compost.

soil color: An indication of how much organic material that soil contains. The darker the color the greater the organic matter content.

soil fertility: A reference to how rich the soil is in nutrients and organic matter.

soil horizon: One of three layers of soil; the soil horizons are topsoil, subsoil, and parent material.

soil structure: The soil's physical condition.

soil test: An analysis of a soil's pH, nutrient content, texture, and other factors.

soil texture: Refers to how much clay, silt, or sand is in the soil.

stolons: Stems that travel just above the surface of the soil.

subshrub: See woody perennial.

subsoil: The second layer, or horizon, of soil. There's less root growth in this layer.

succession planting: Growing one crop after another so that the garden is in use for the entire growing season. Often used in vegetable gardening.

surface horizon: See topsoil.

synthetic fertilizer: Manmade, nonorganic fertilizer.

tender annuals: Annuals that don't tolerate the cold and will be killed by frost.

tender perennials: Perennials that won't survive the winter in certain climates and that need to be lifted and stored in cold weather to be replanted in the spring.

thatch: A buildup of organic matter comprising dead and dying stems and roots that settles on the soil surface and interferes with the growth of turfgrass.

thinning: A pruning term that refers to taking entire limbs out from the bottom or back to the trunk.

till: Soil that is a mix of sand, silt, and clay.

tillers: New shoots that form at the base of a plant near the soil.

tilth: See soil structure.

topping: A pruning term that refers to the removal of part of a limb probably closer to the end of the limb. Also known as *heading.*

topsoil: The first layer or surface horizon of soil. It is usually darker because of the organic content. It is in this layer that most of the root action takes place so plants obtain most of their water and nutrients from this surface horizon.

trunk flare: The area where a tree's roots meet the trunk. Also called the root collar or root flare.

viral disease: Disease caused by a virus. The entire plant may be stunted in growth and misshapen with yellowing leaves that are mottled and curling with no visible veins.

warm-weather crops: Crops that grow better in warmer temperatures and so are planted later in the season.

woody perennial: A plant with woody, stiff stems that does not die back to its crown or roots. Often referred to as a subshrub.

xeriscaping: A term for landscaping that uses indigenous and drought-tolerant plants.

Index

I

insecticidal soap, 149
insecticides, 149–50
insects, 141–44
  beneficial, 142–44
  life cycle of, 140–41
integrated disease management (IDM), 136
integrated pest management (IPM), 136–41
interplanting, 91
invasive plants, 123–33, 172–74
  disposal of, 131
  eradicating, 128–31
  plant list, 125
  substitutes for, 132–33
irrigation zones. *See* watering
Islands, the, 6–7

K

Kane, Tim, 52
kettle holes, 7
Kiely, Jim, 94–96
Kyker-Snowman, Thomas, 123–124

L

Langh, Ruth, 75–76
lawn, 109–22
  diseases, 121–22
  fertilizing, 117
  maintaining, 116–17
  mowing, 116

rhizomes, 110
stolons, 110
weeds, 119
lime, 10–11
loam, 9

M

MacFadyen, Crisse, 30
Mahoney, Mike, 54, 56
manure, 15
Marcellot, Judy, 77
Marcellot, Michel, 70
master gardener hotlines, 164–65
Maynard, Brian, 102, 149
Mellor, David, 120
Mezitt, Wayne, 65
microclimates, 30–31, 154
milky disease (Milky Spore), 118, 149
Miskovsky, Paul, 5, 28, 45
Morris, Julie, 101
mulch, 59, 61
Murray, Mike, 16, 116

N

native plants. *See* invasive plants
neem, 150
nematodes, 118
New England Rose Society, 171
New England Wild Flower Society, 165
Novak, James, 109, 111, 113

nutrients, 13–14
　deficiencies, 138

O

organic fertilizers, 15
organic matter, 14, 43–44

P

parent material, 8
Paxton soil, 5
perennials, 63–79
　acquiring, 71–72
　care of, 72–73
　half-hardy, 65
　hardy, 64
　herbaceous, 63
　maintenance, 77–79
　semihardy, 65
　tender, 65
　transplanting, 71–72
　woody, 63–64
pesticides, 149–50
pests, 136–44
　common, 148–49
　control of, 140–44
　identifying, 139
　life cycle, 140
pH (potential hydrogen), 9–11
　changing, 10
　plant preferences, 11
plant nutrition, 13–17
pollinators, 142–43
pot bound, 100
predators, 142–43
Provest, Barbara, 66

pruning, 104–6
public gardens, 166–68
pyrethrin, 150

R

rain barrels, 36
rain data, 33
Rawson, Julie, 25, 84, 90
Rocheleau, Mike, 19
roses, 64
Rotenone, 150
runoff, 42

S

Sachs, Paul, 112
seaside gardens, 159–62
　designing, 159
Shane, Mary, 46
Shepherd, Renee, 85
shrubs. *See* trees
Simmons, Tim, 129
site, 21–32
soaker hoses, 40
sod, 115
soils, 2–32
　acid, 9–10
　alkaline, 9–10
　amendments, 14–17, 43
　clay, 3, 11
　color, 8
　Paxton soil, 5
　properties of, 7
　sandy, 3
　silty, 4
　soil test, 12–13

About the Author

Barbara Gee is a regional editor of the Northeast magazine *People, Places & Plants* and a contributing writer on gardening for *Yankee, Newport Life,* and *Cambridge Life* magazines. A former Brookline resident, she received her master gardener certification in Rhode Island, studied with the British Royal Horticultural Society, and has worked in the department of horticulture at Blithewold Mansion, Gardens & Arboretum in Rhode Island.